HAPPY FISH

COLORING BOOK

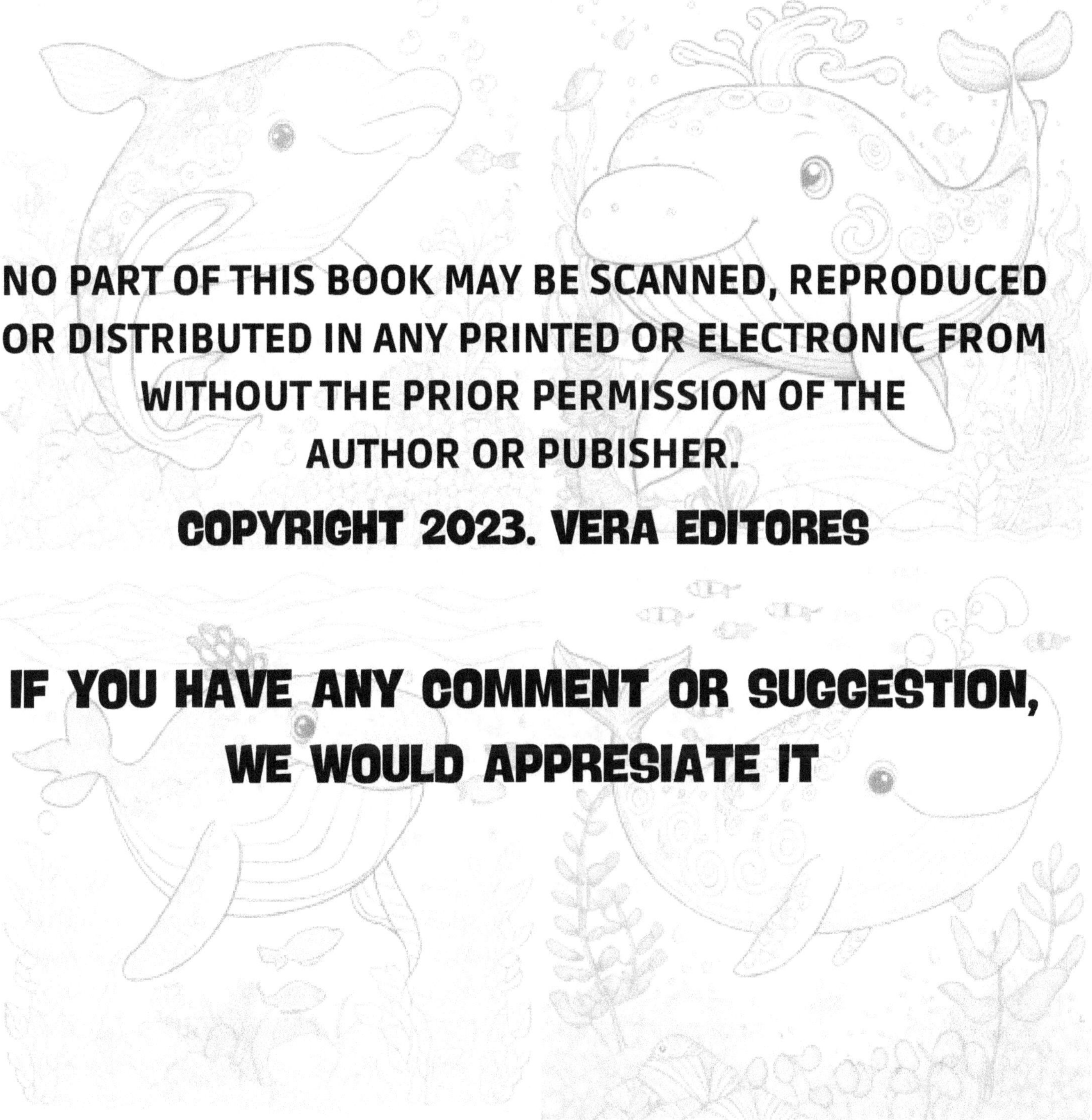

IF YOU HAVE ANY COMMENT OR SUGGESTION, WE WOULD APPRESIATE IT

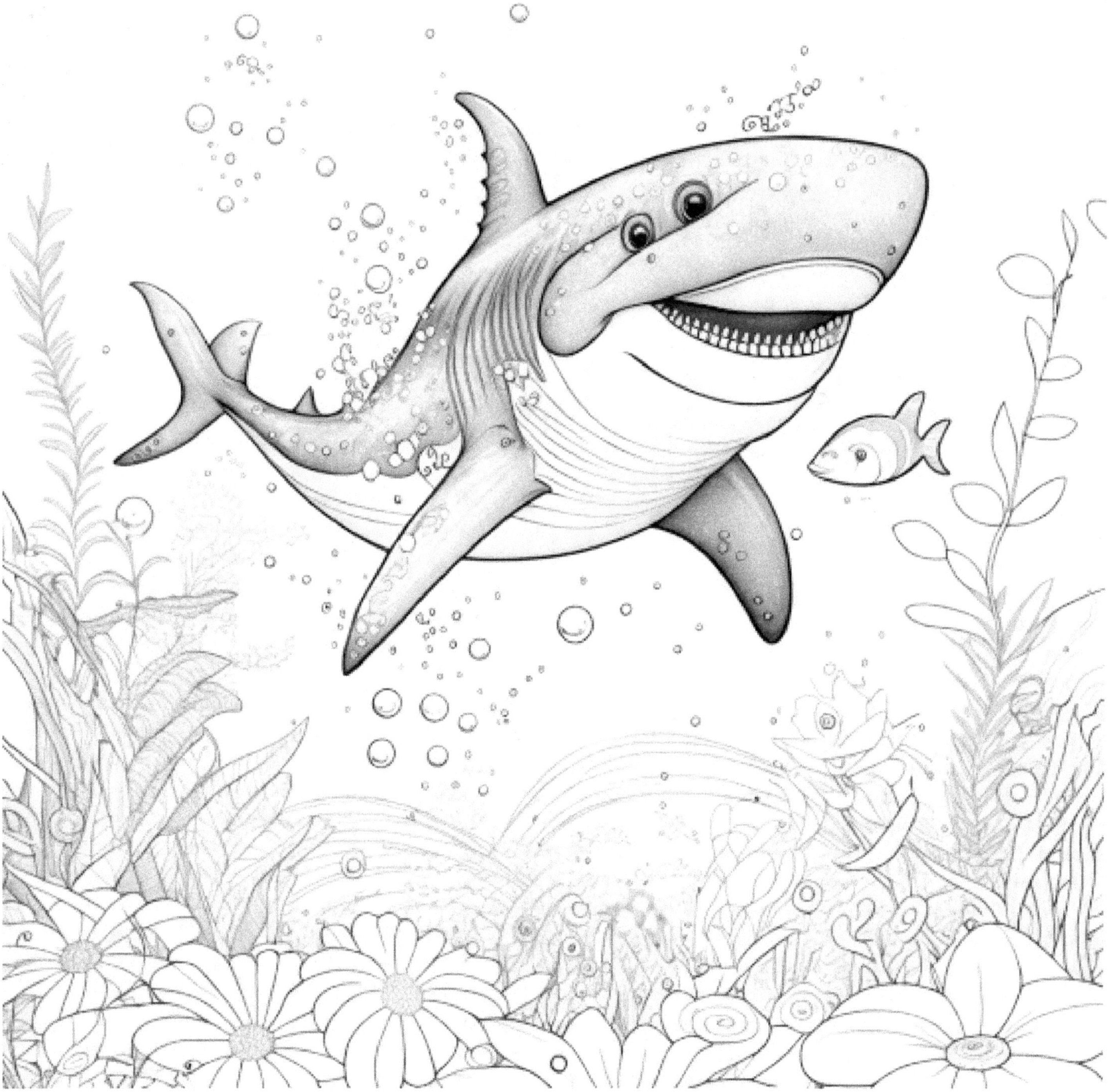

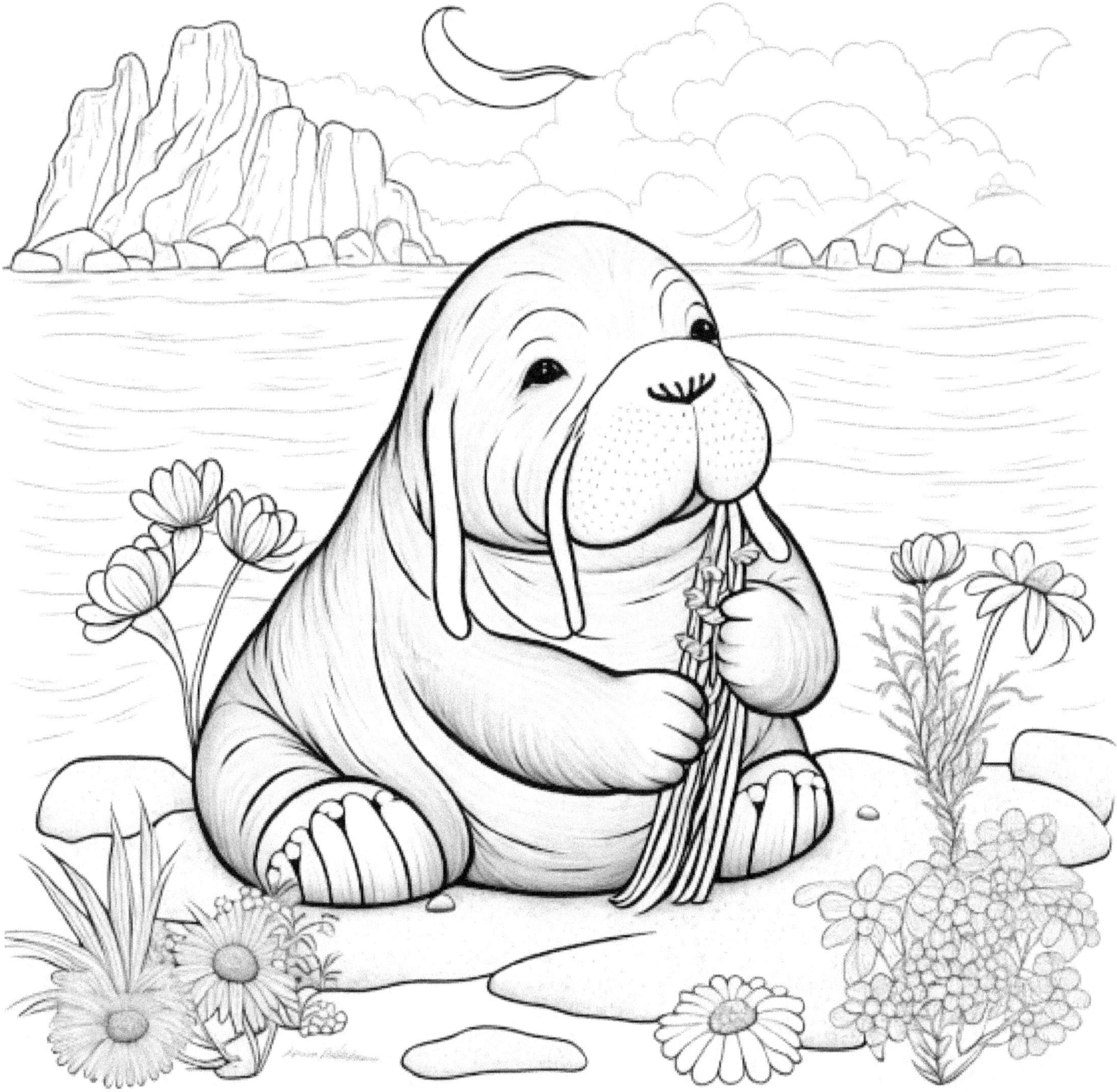

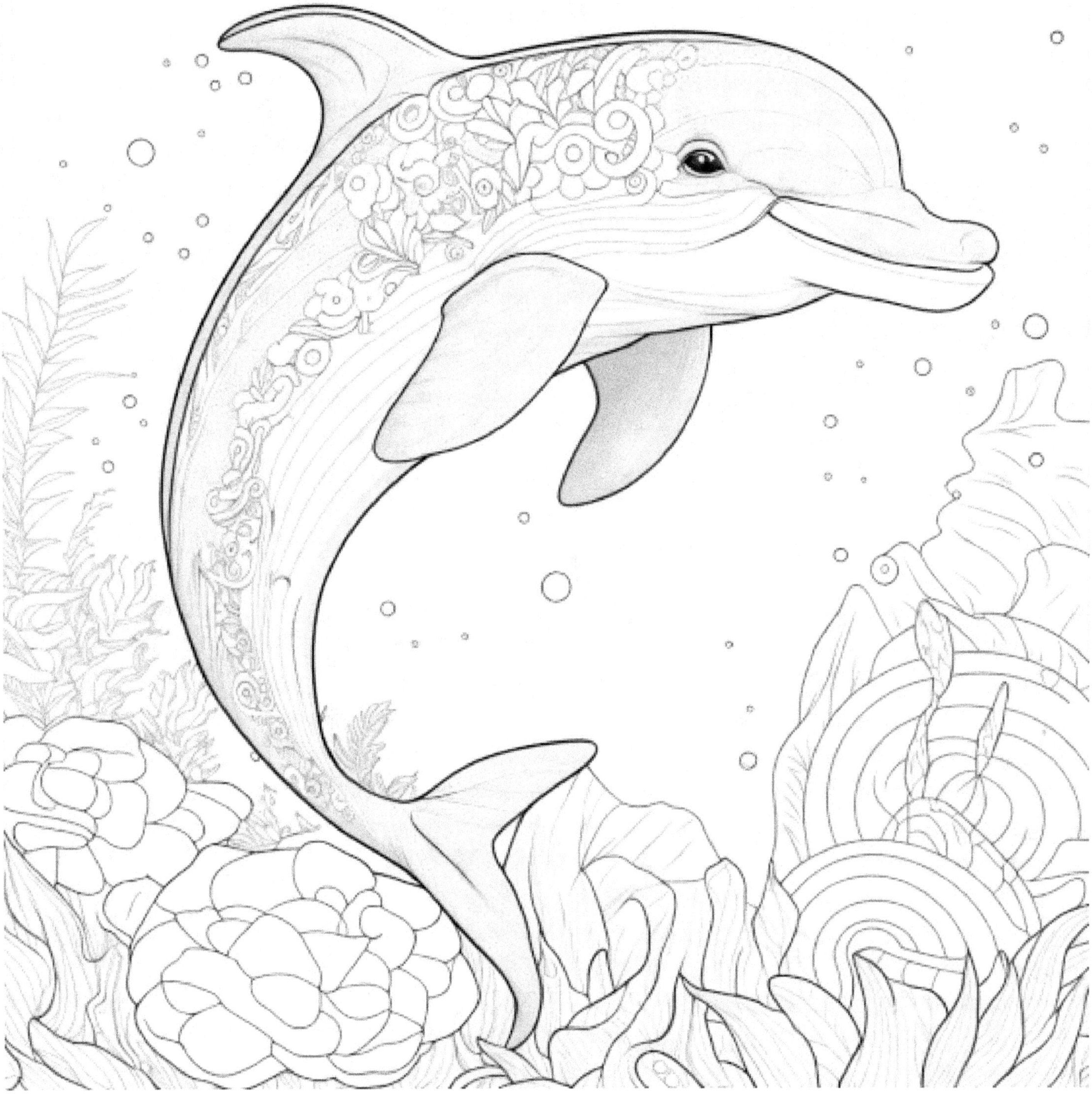

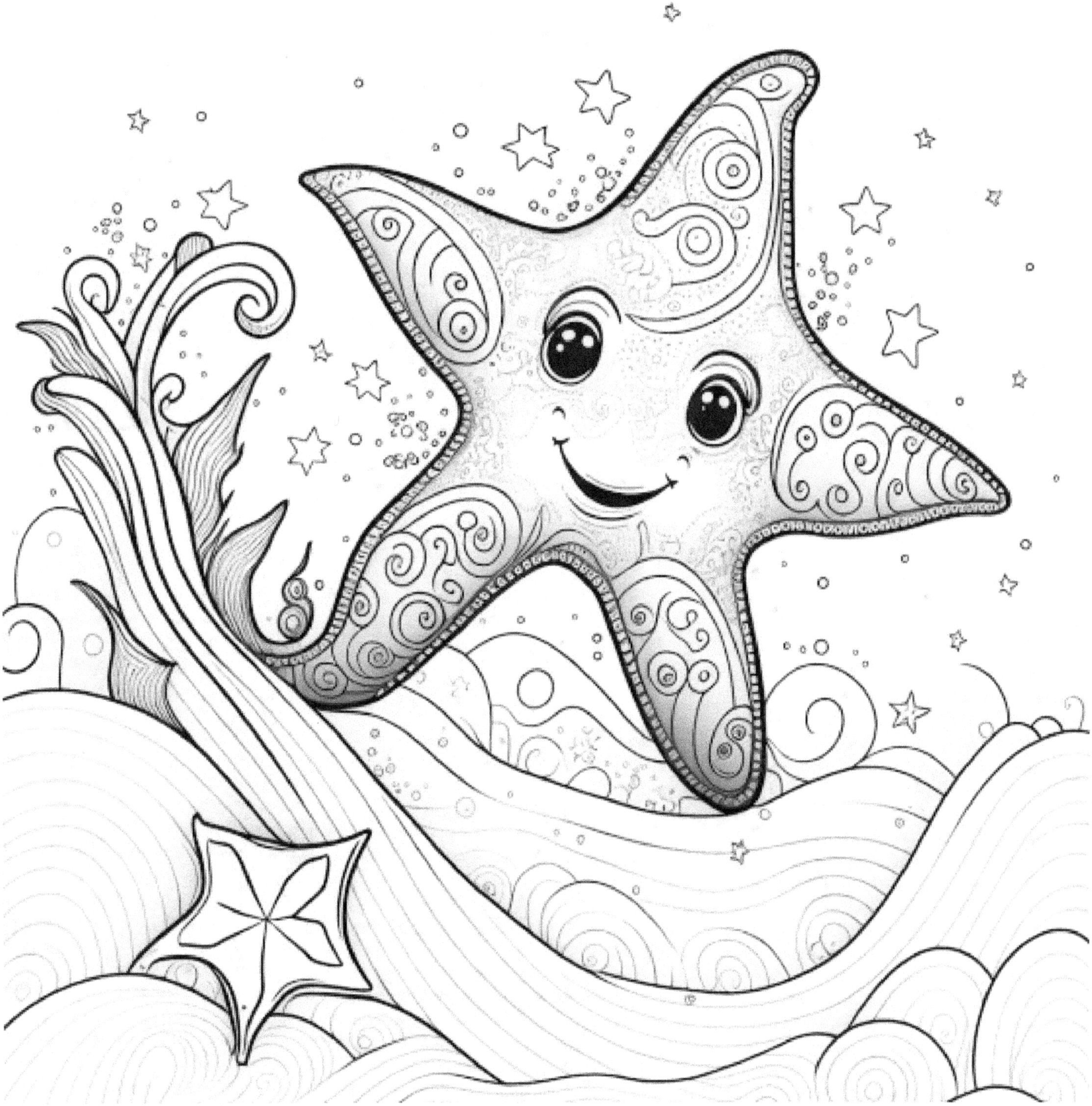

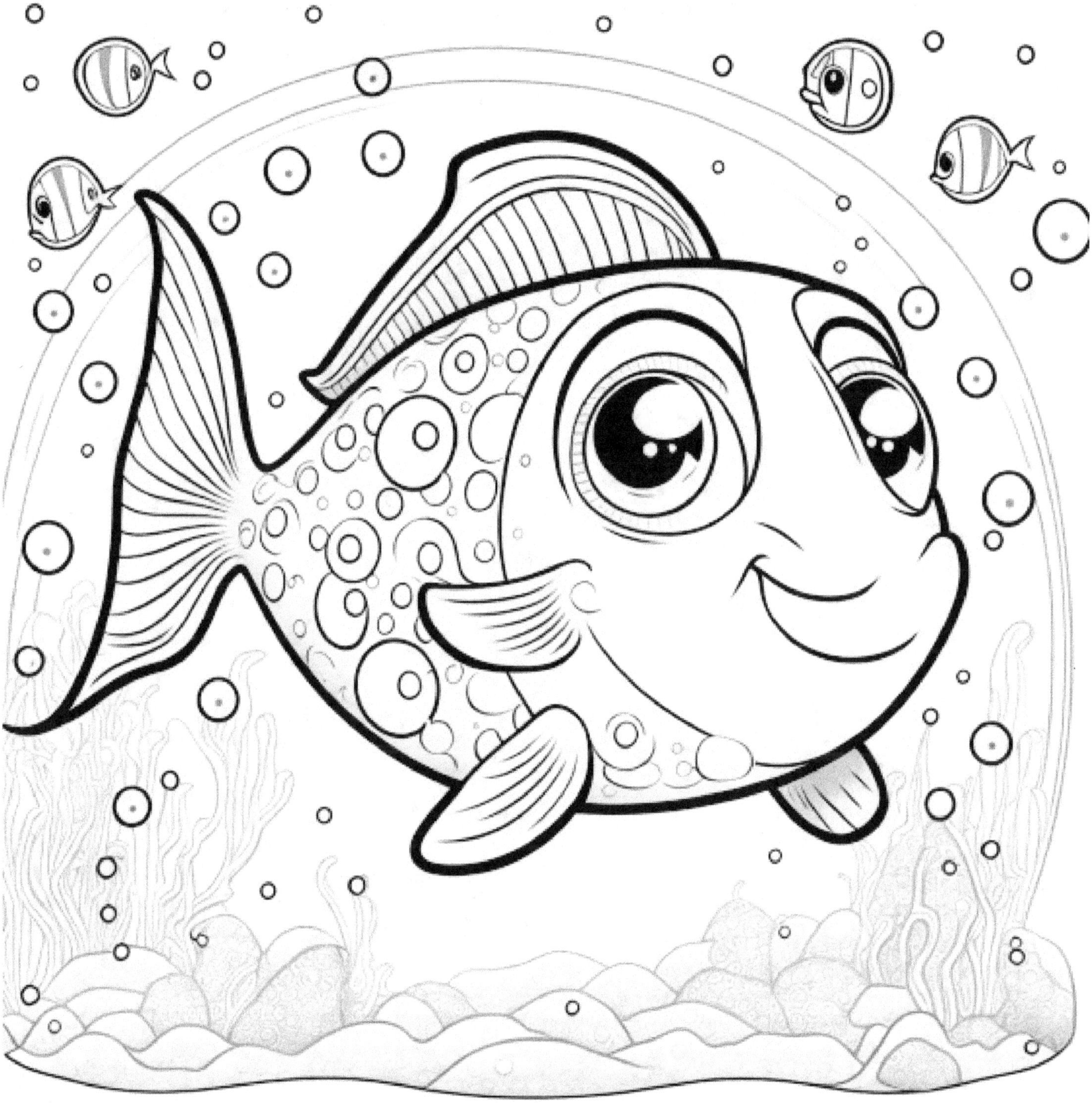

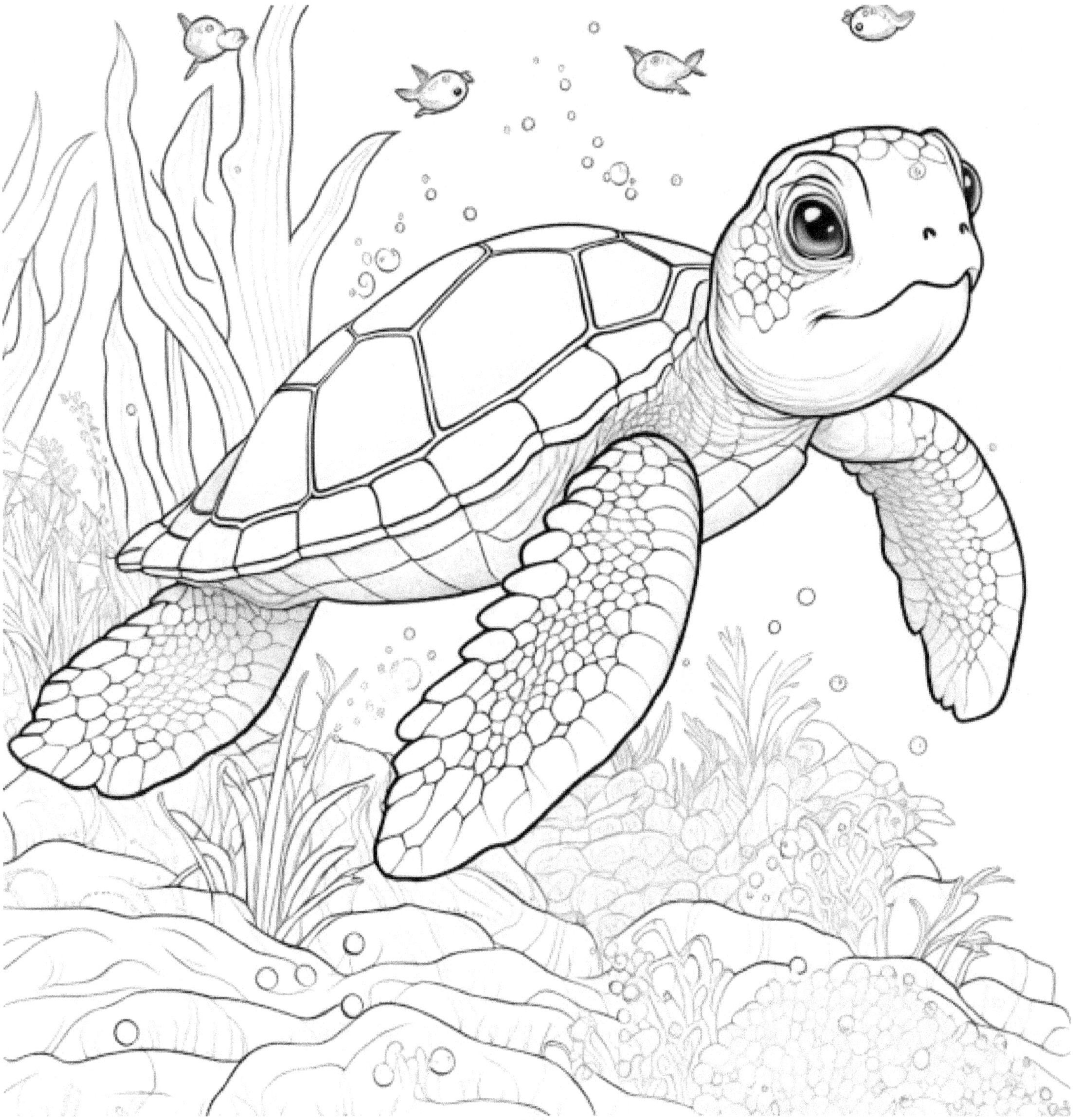

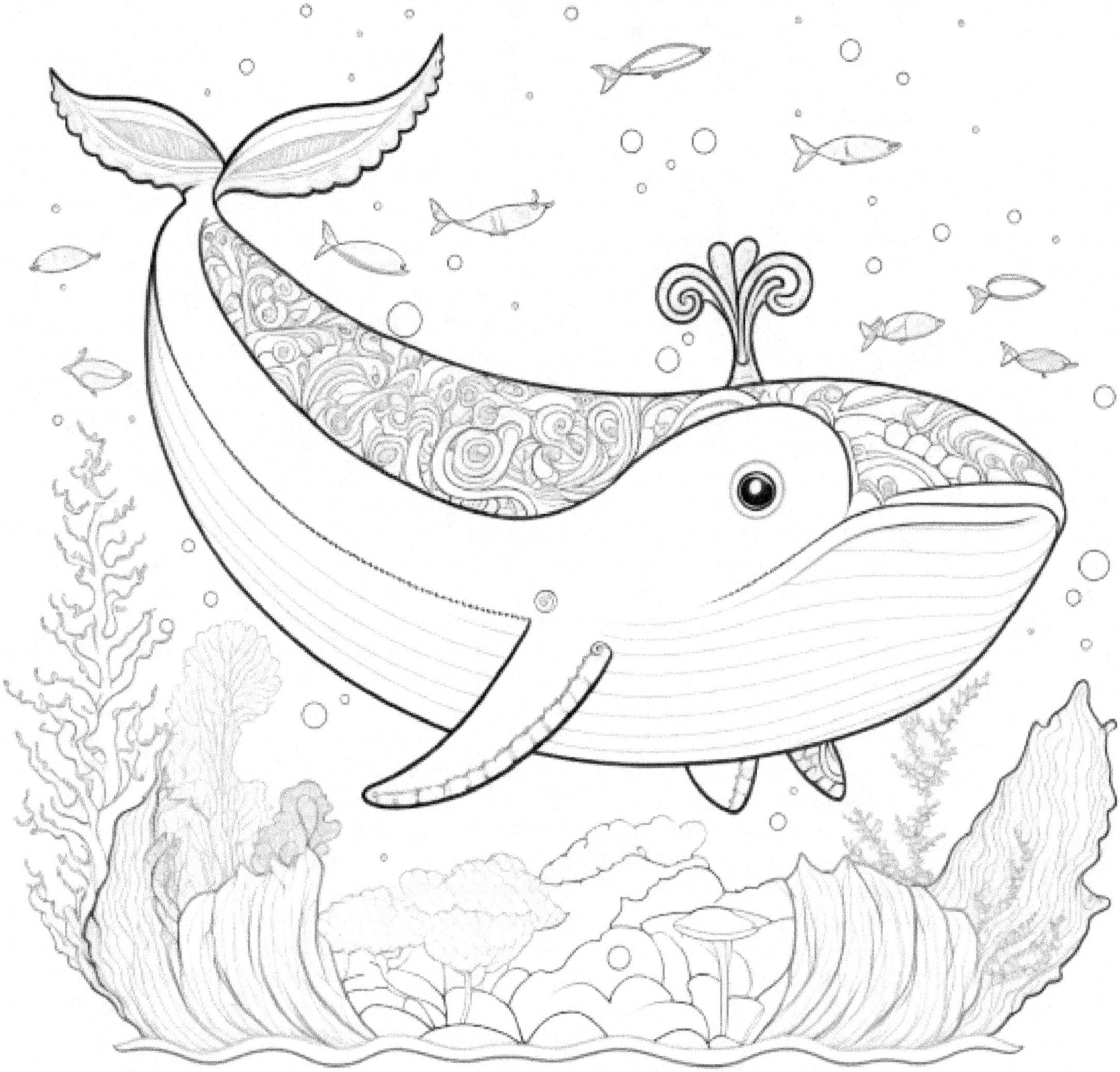

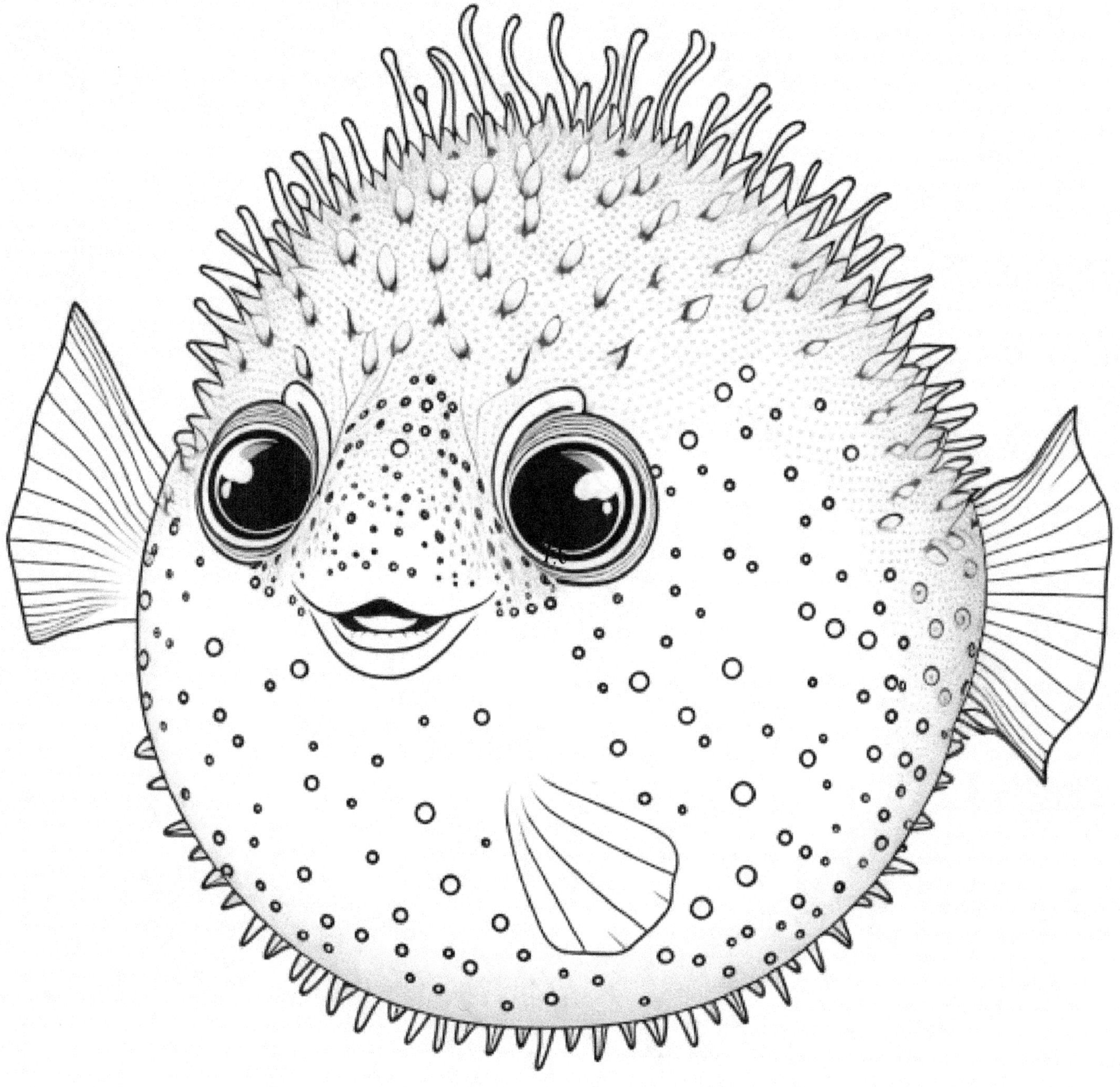

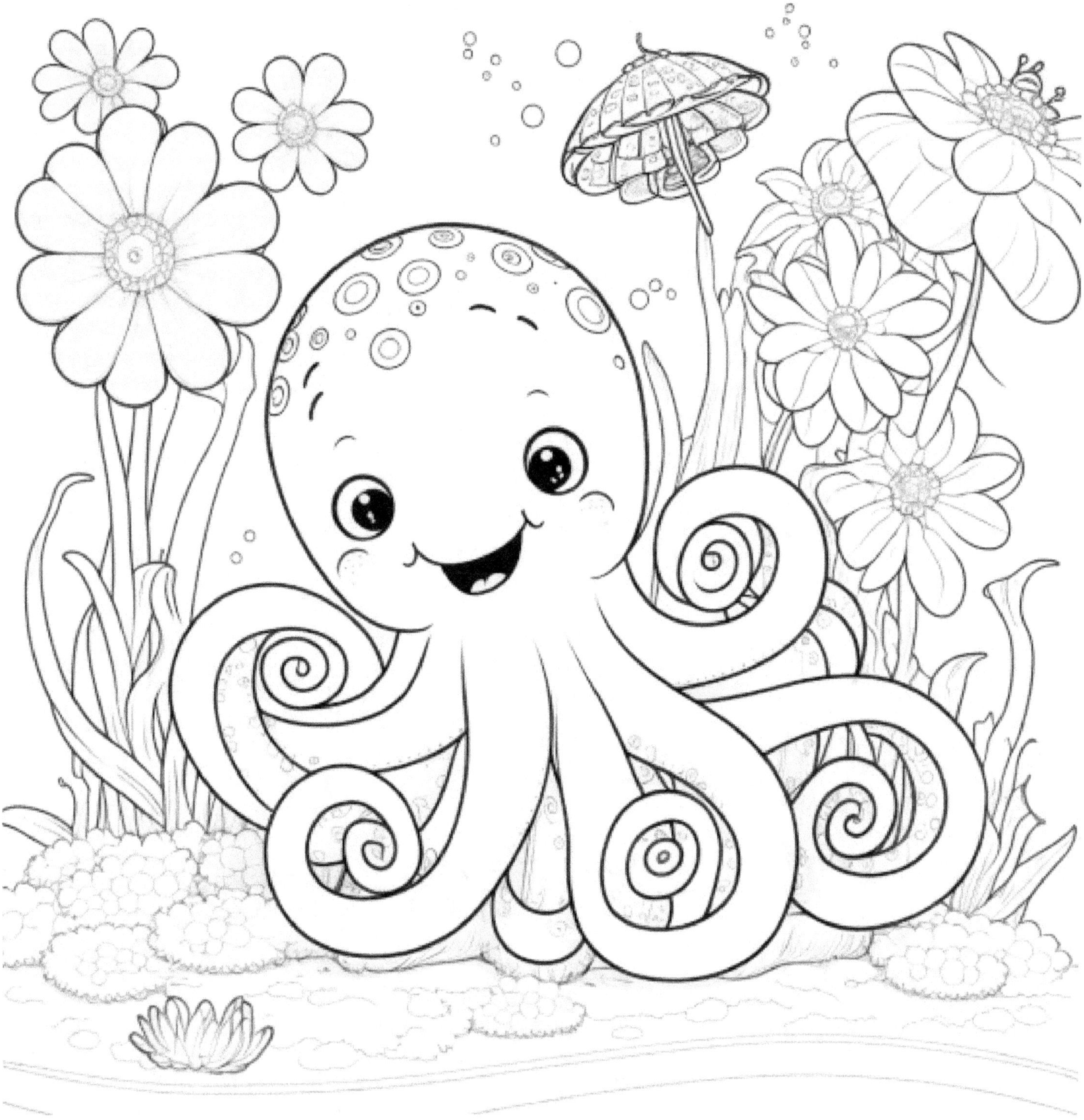

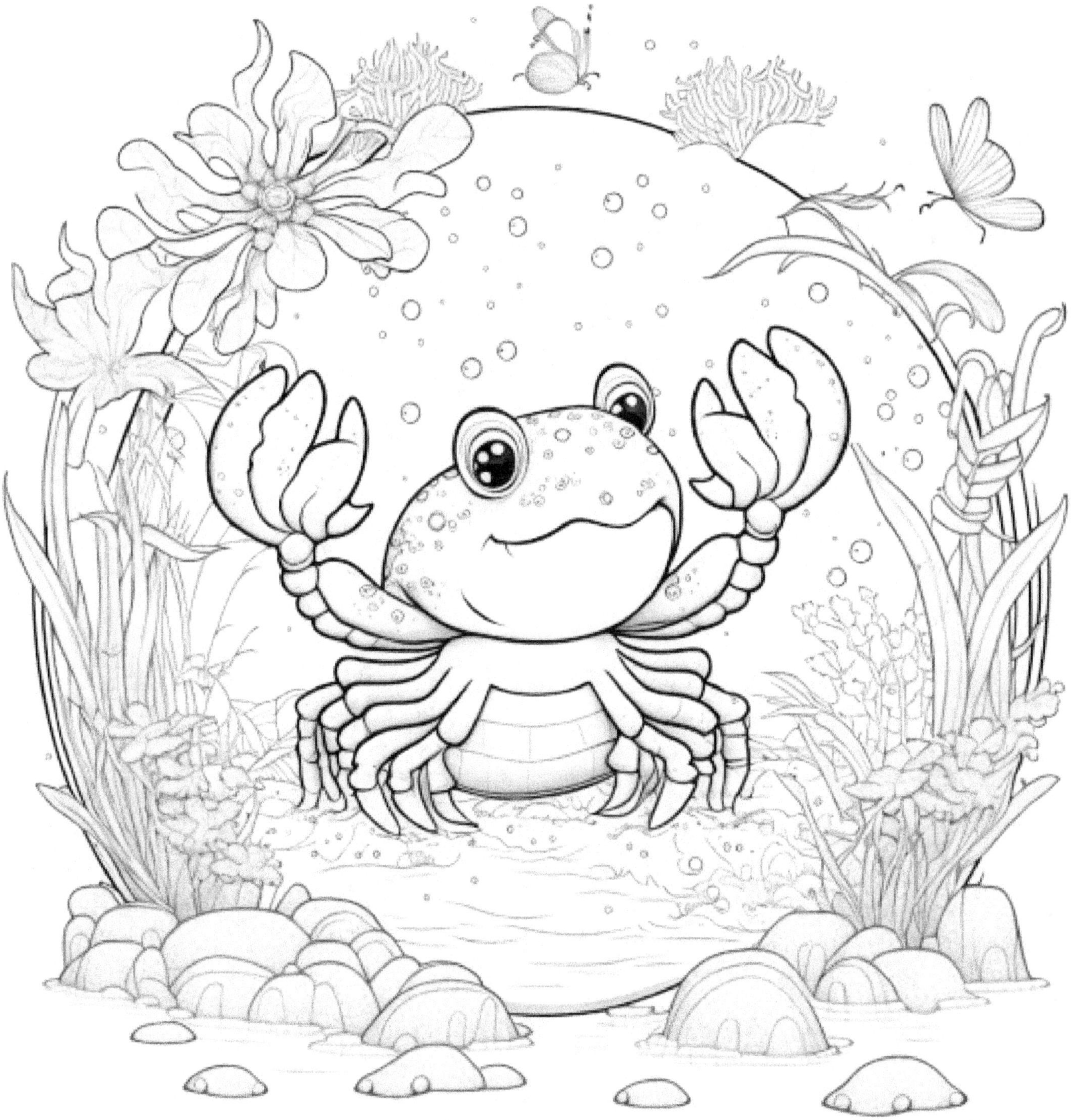

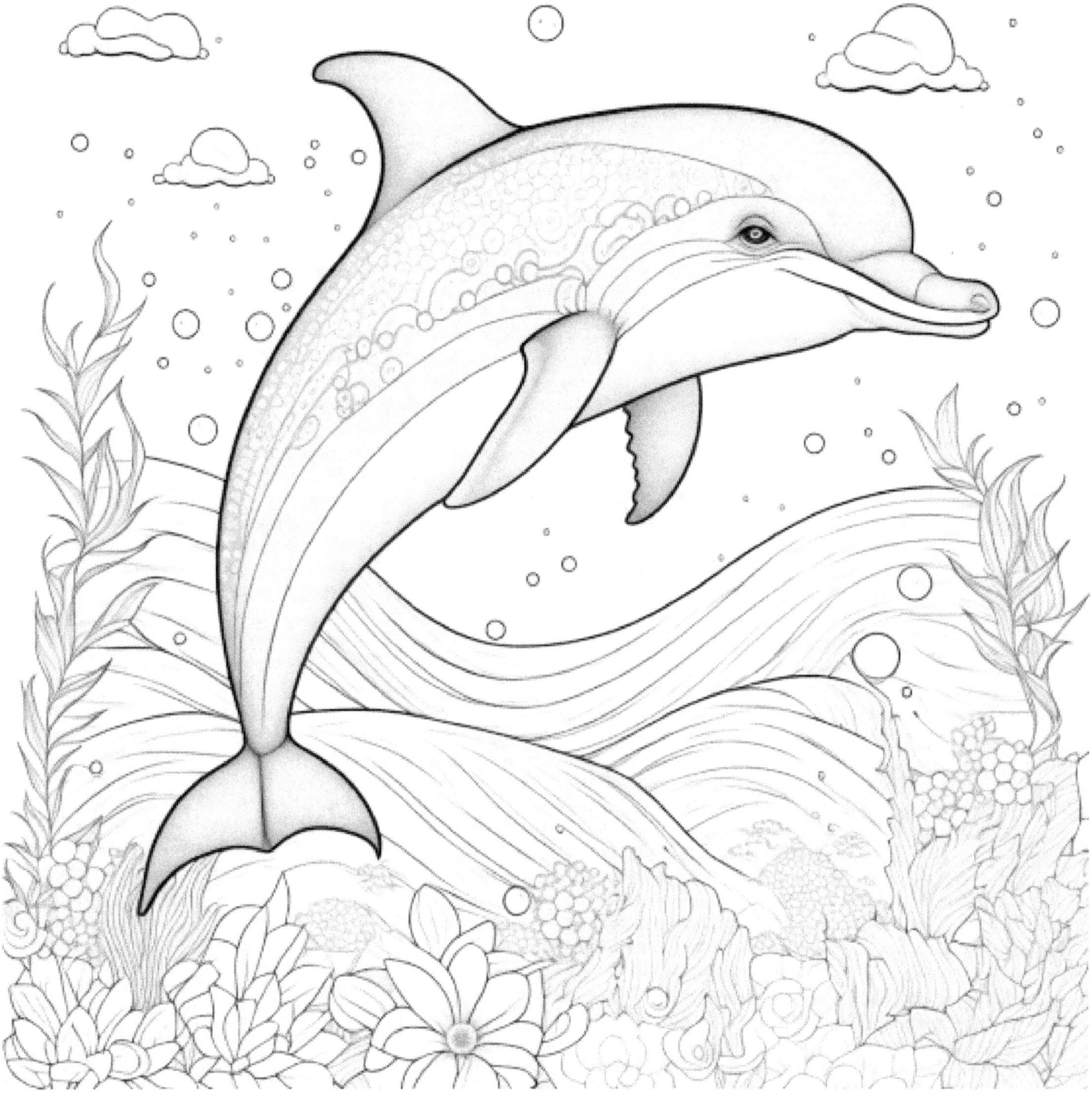

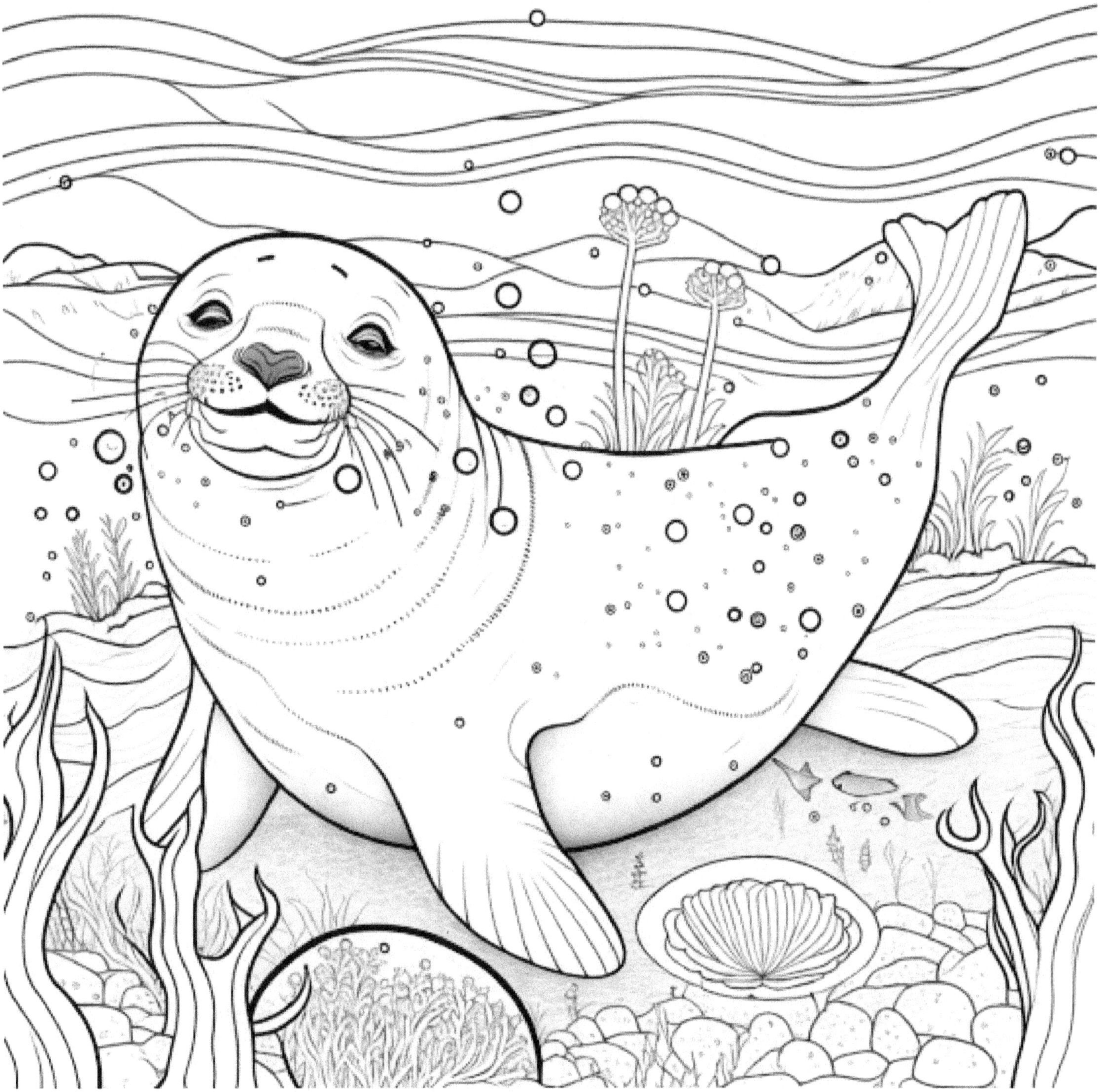

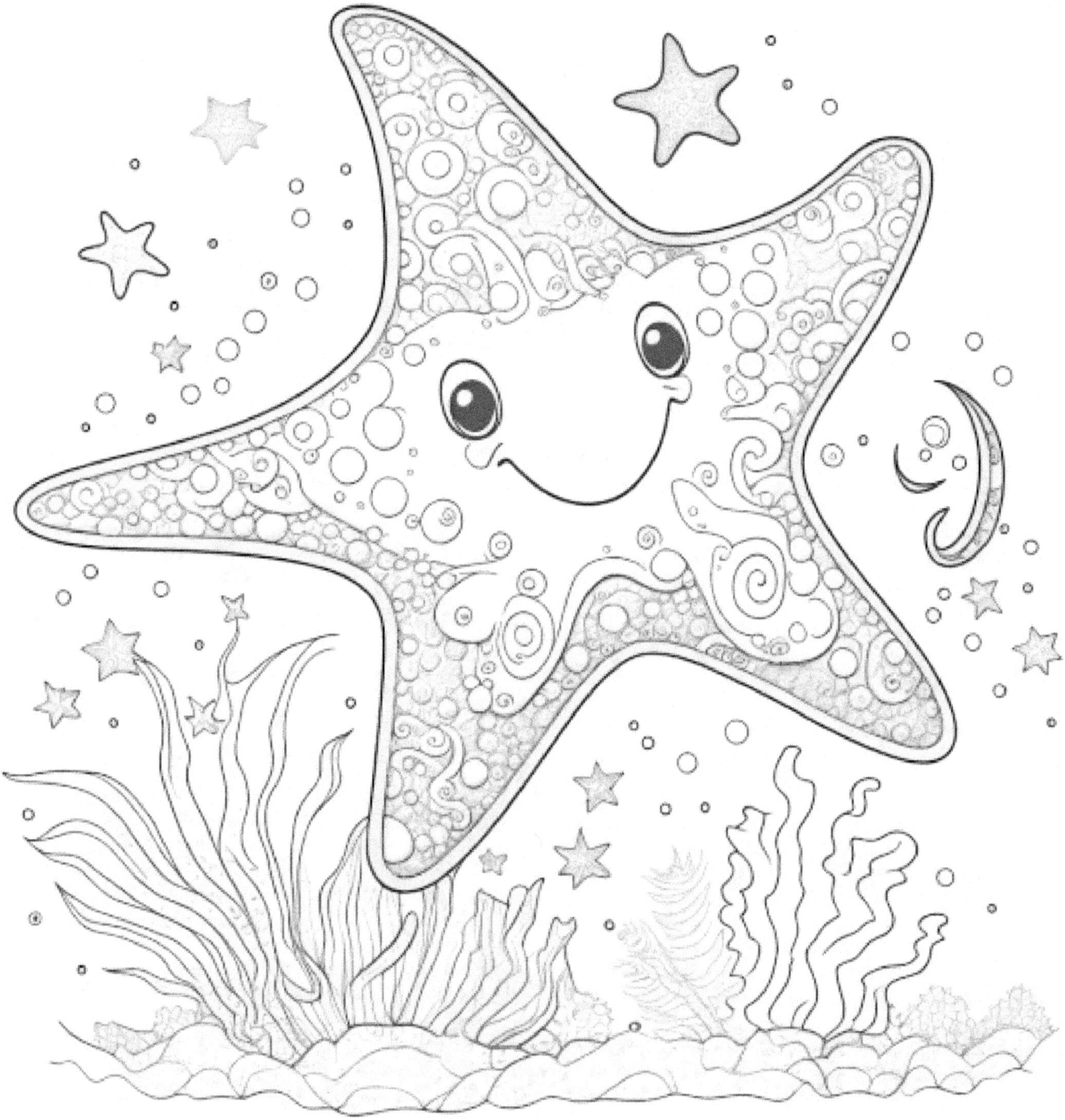

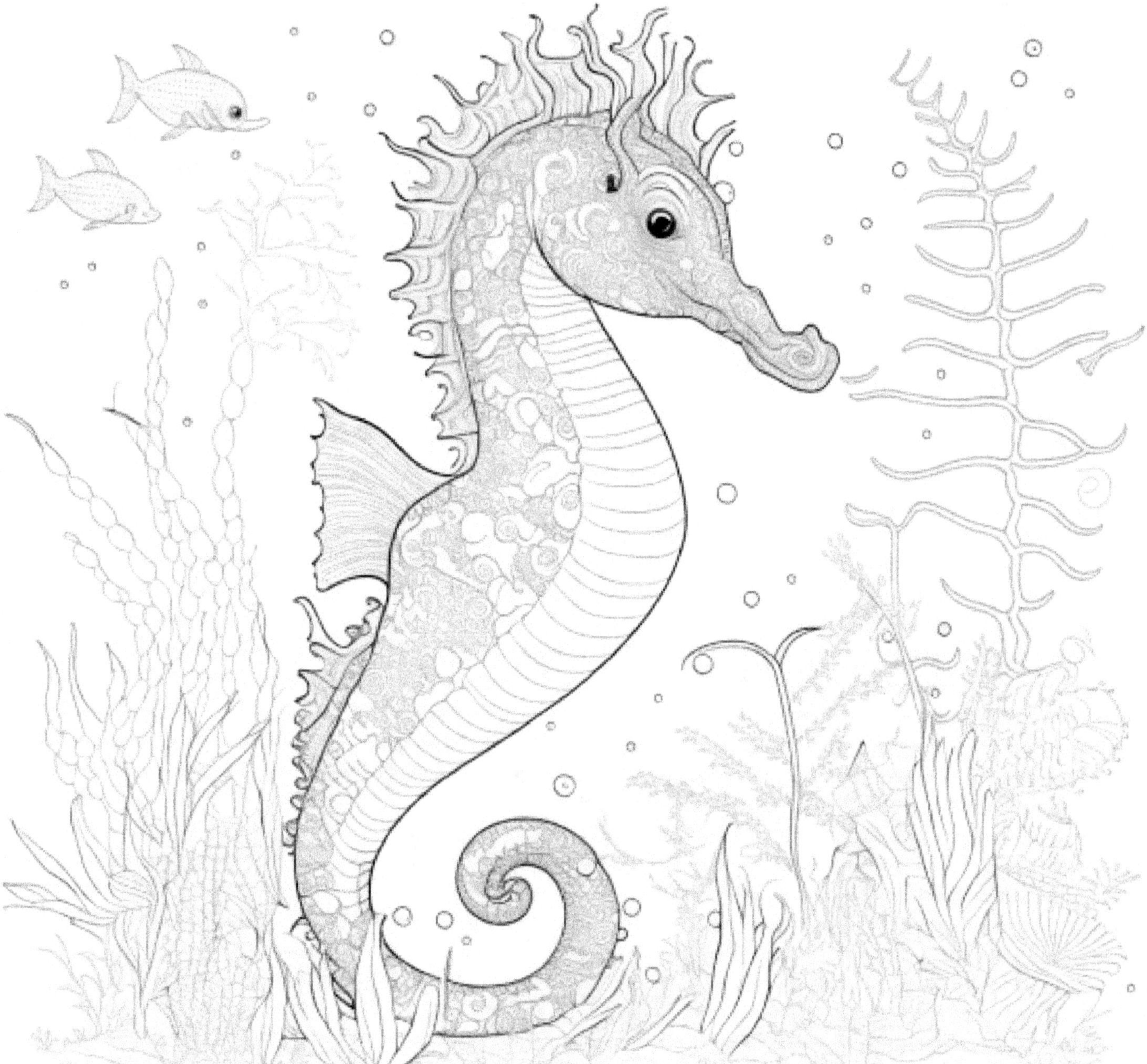

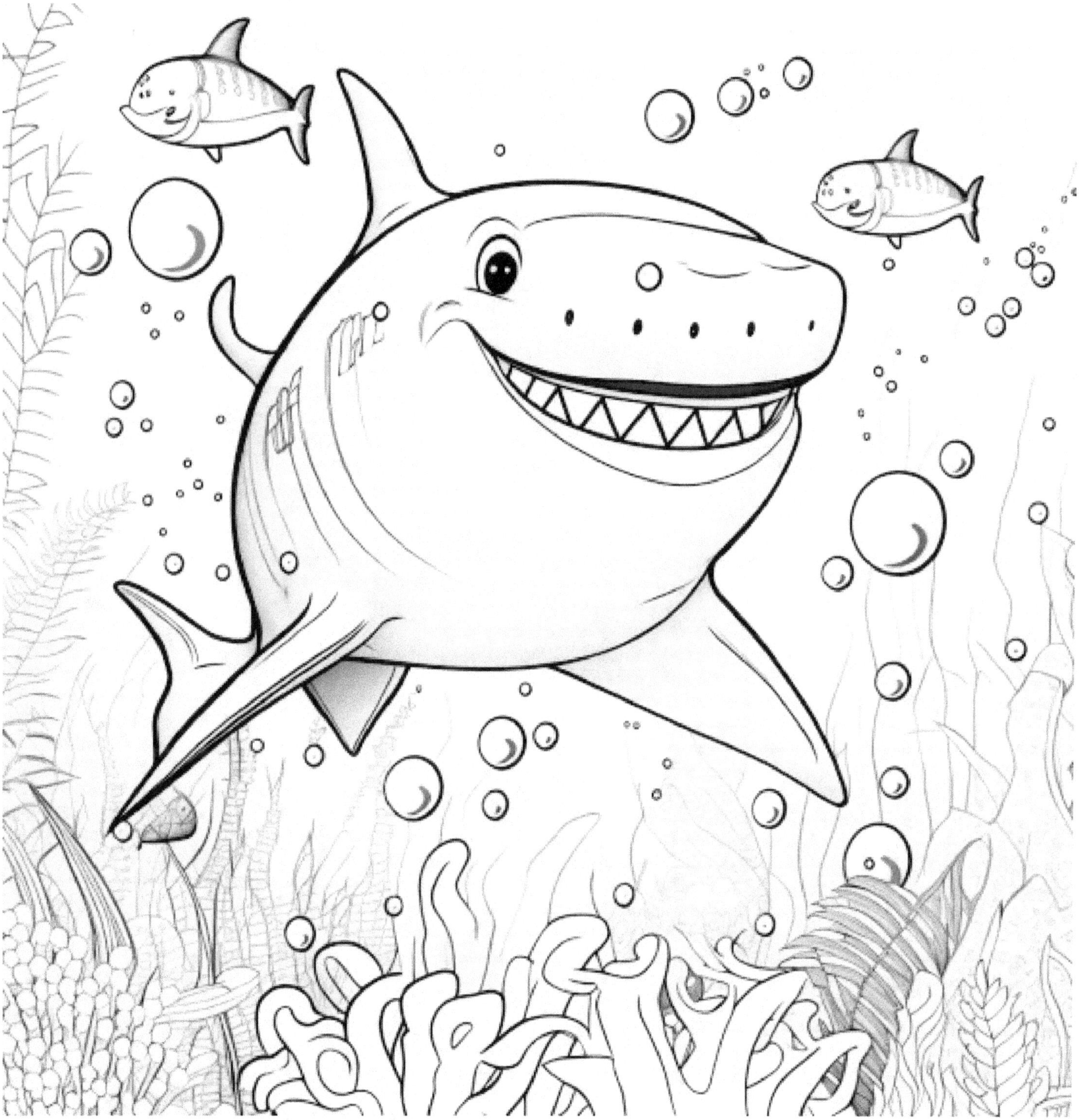

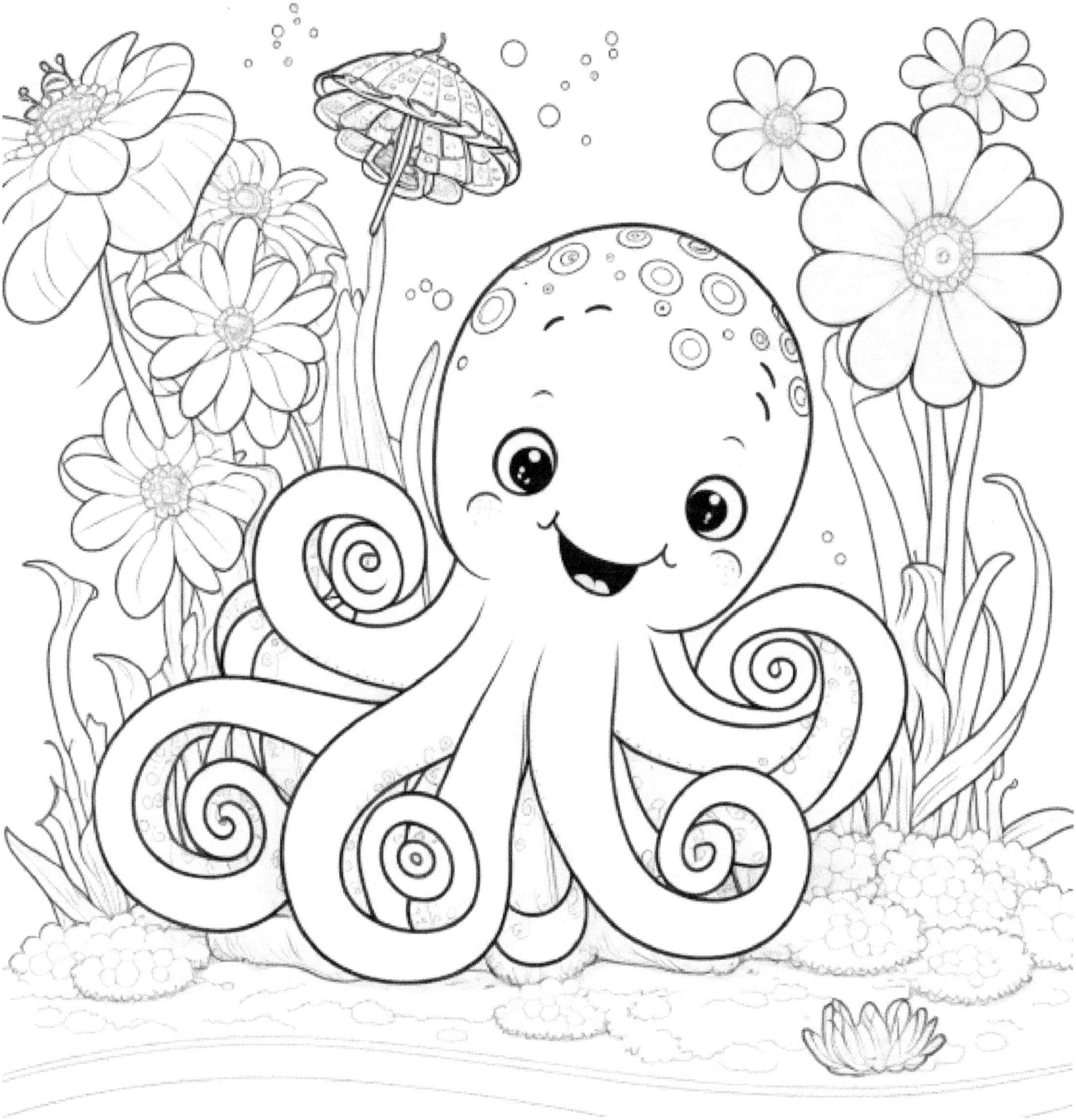

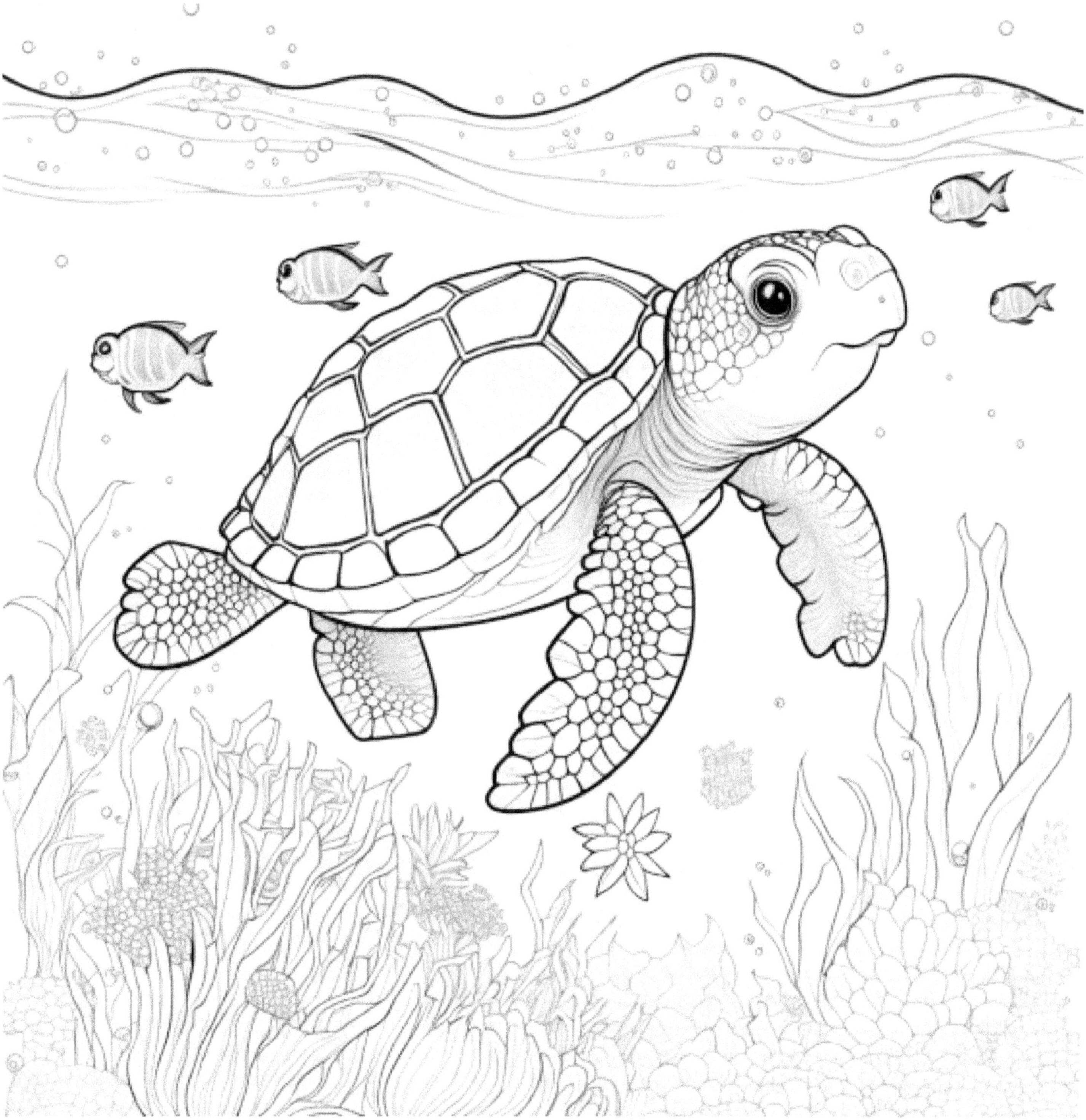

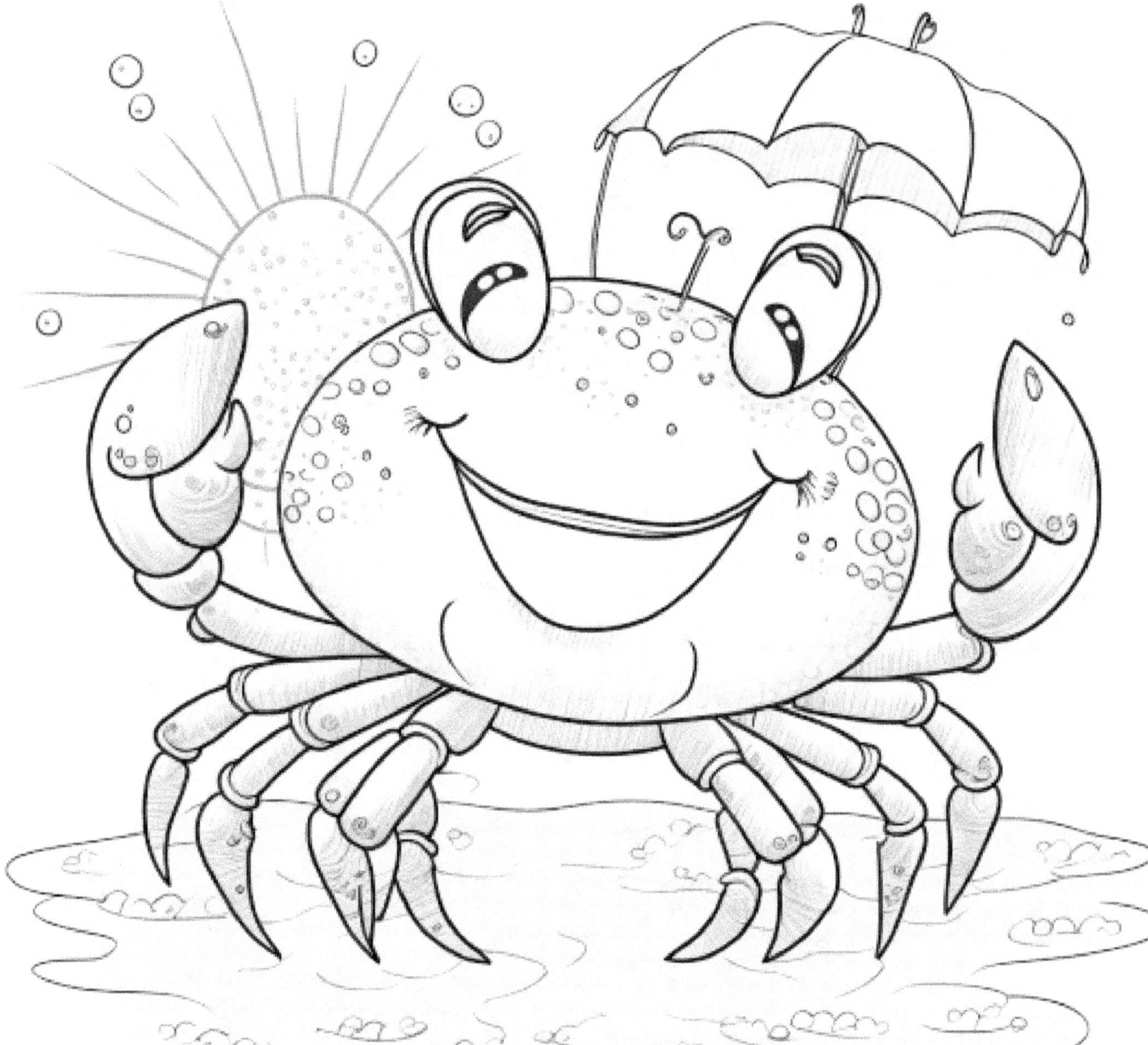

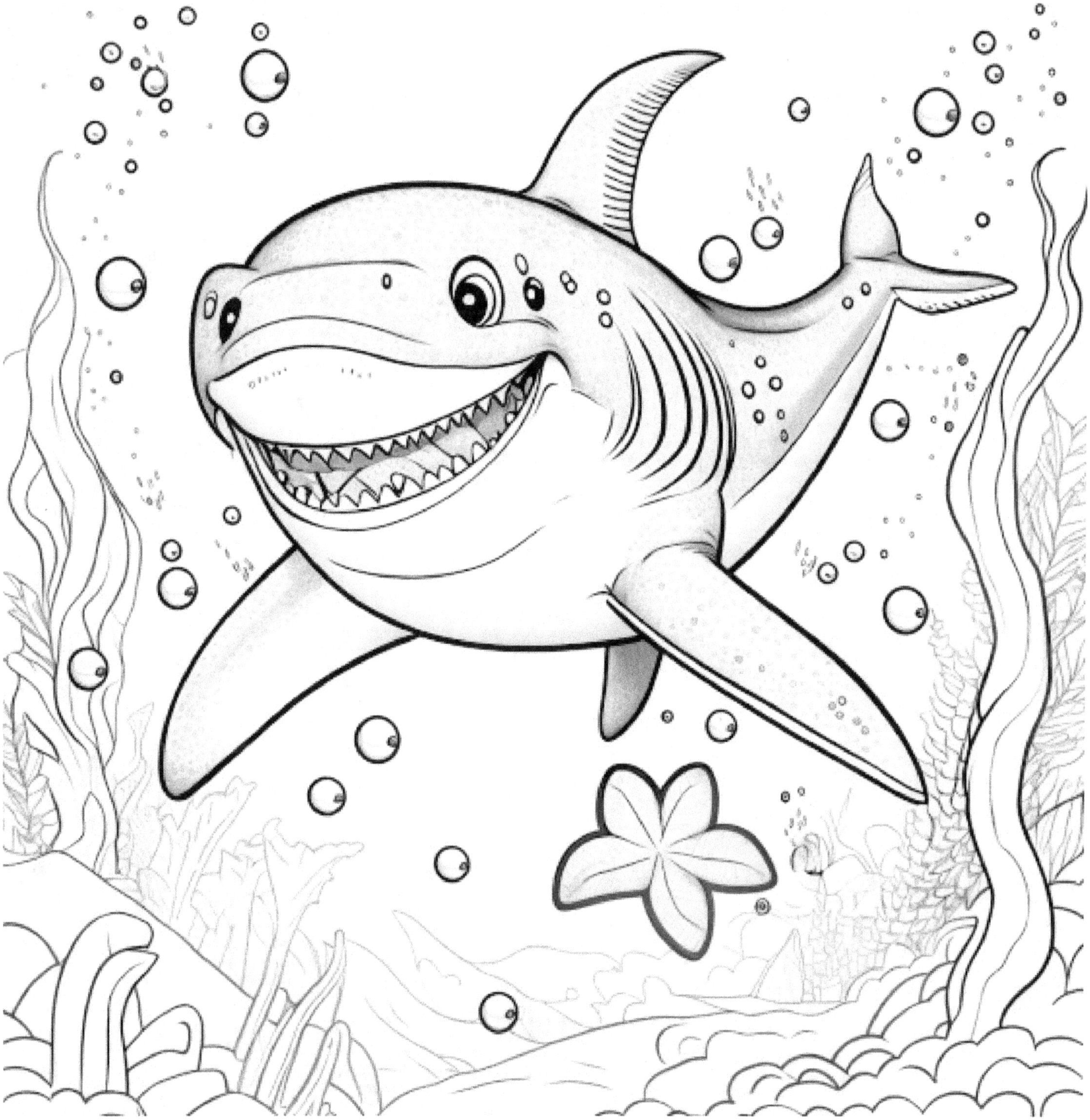

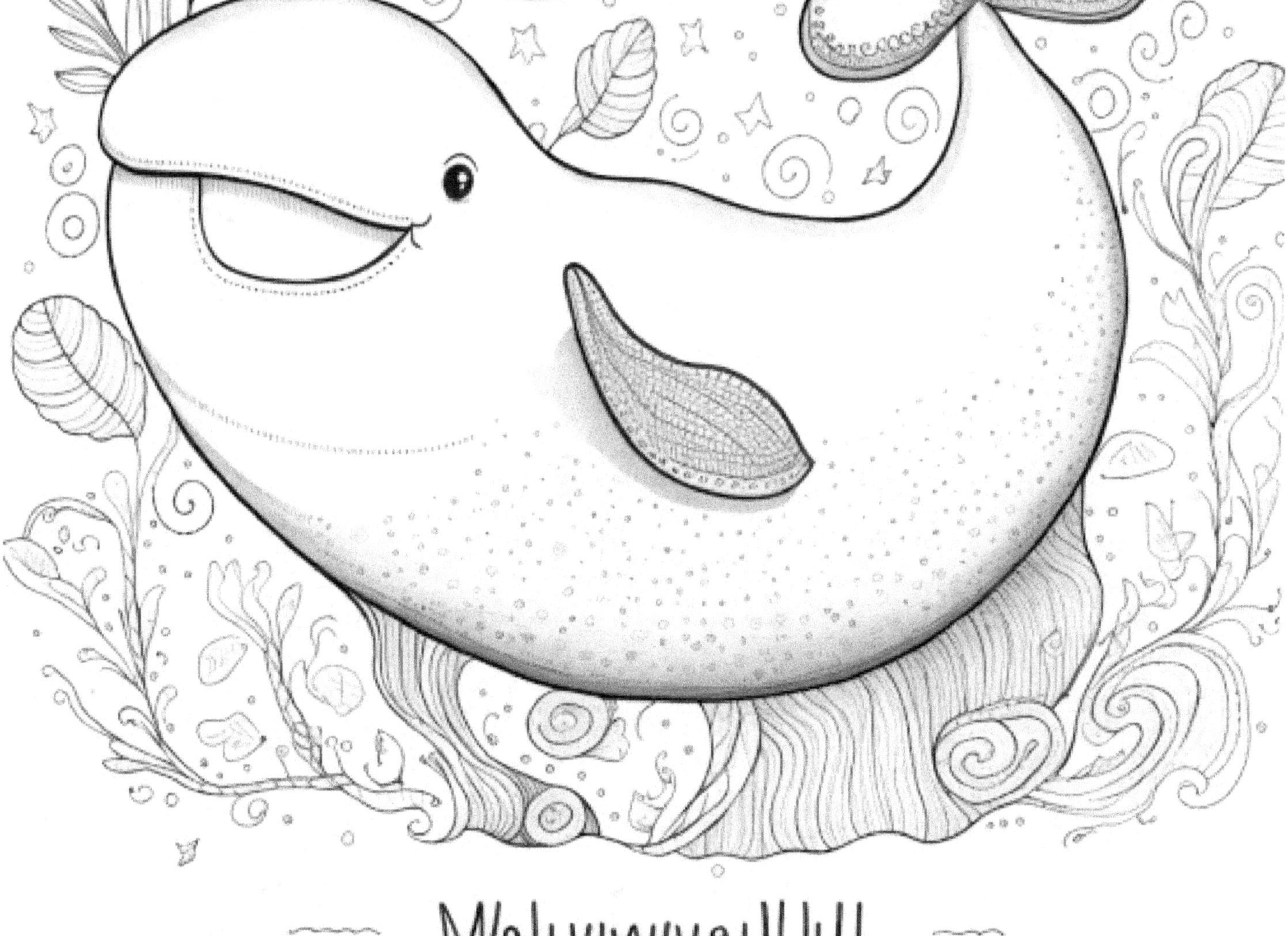

Walıvıwıvaıllılll.

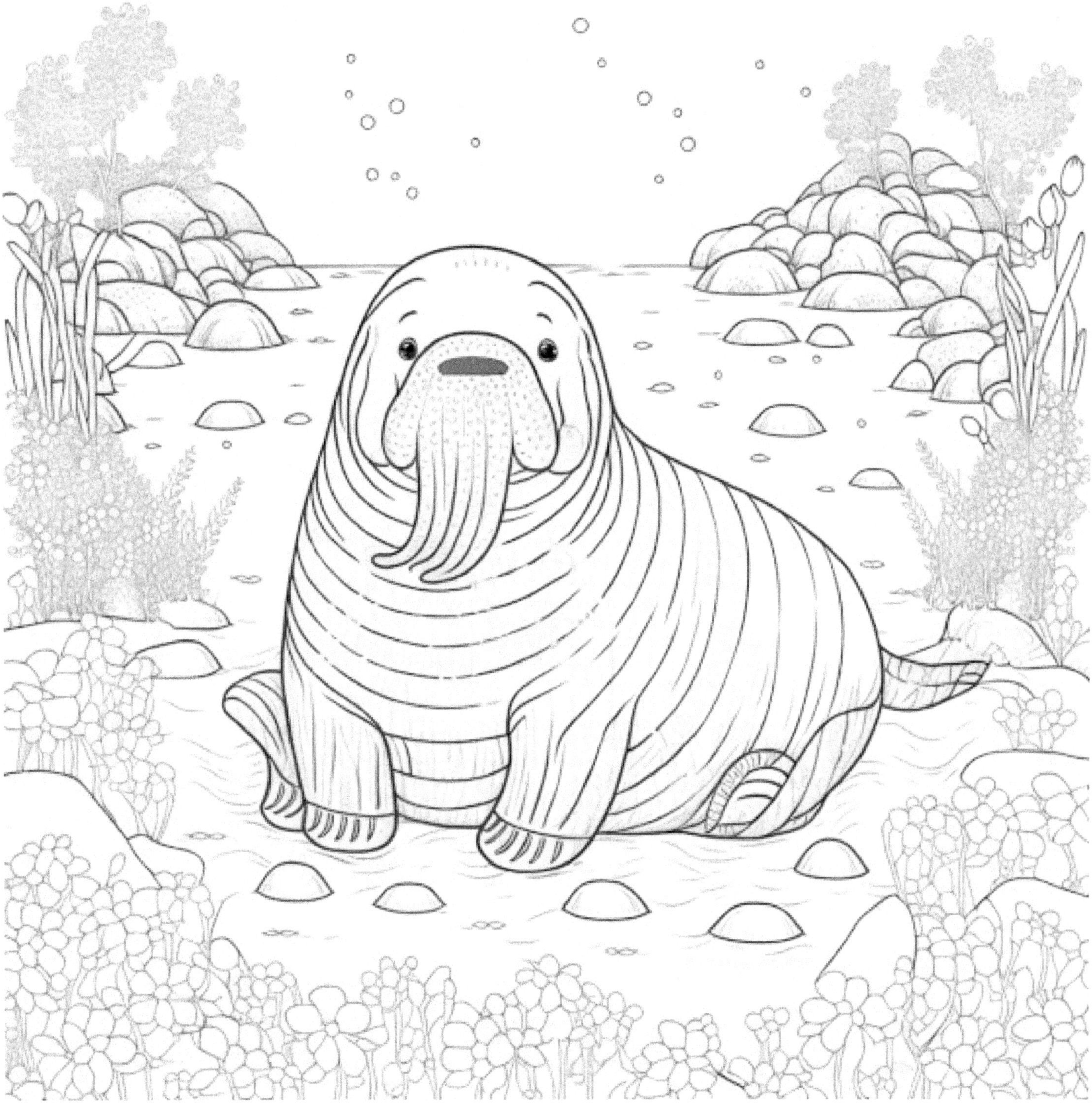

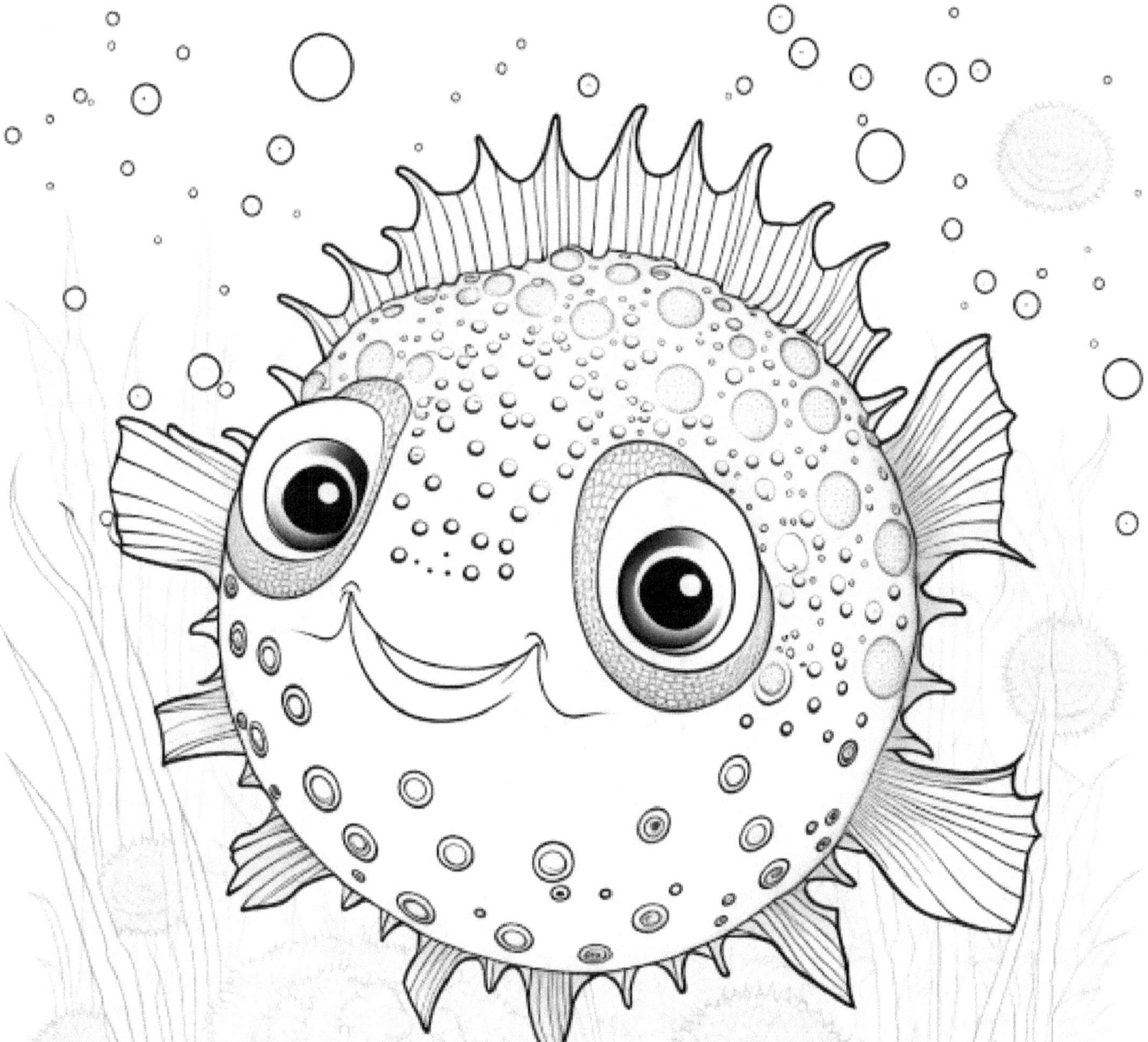

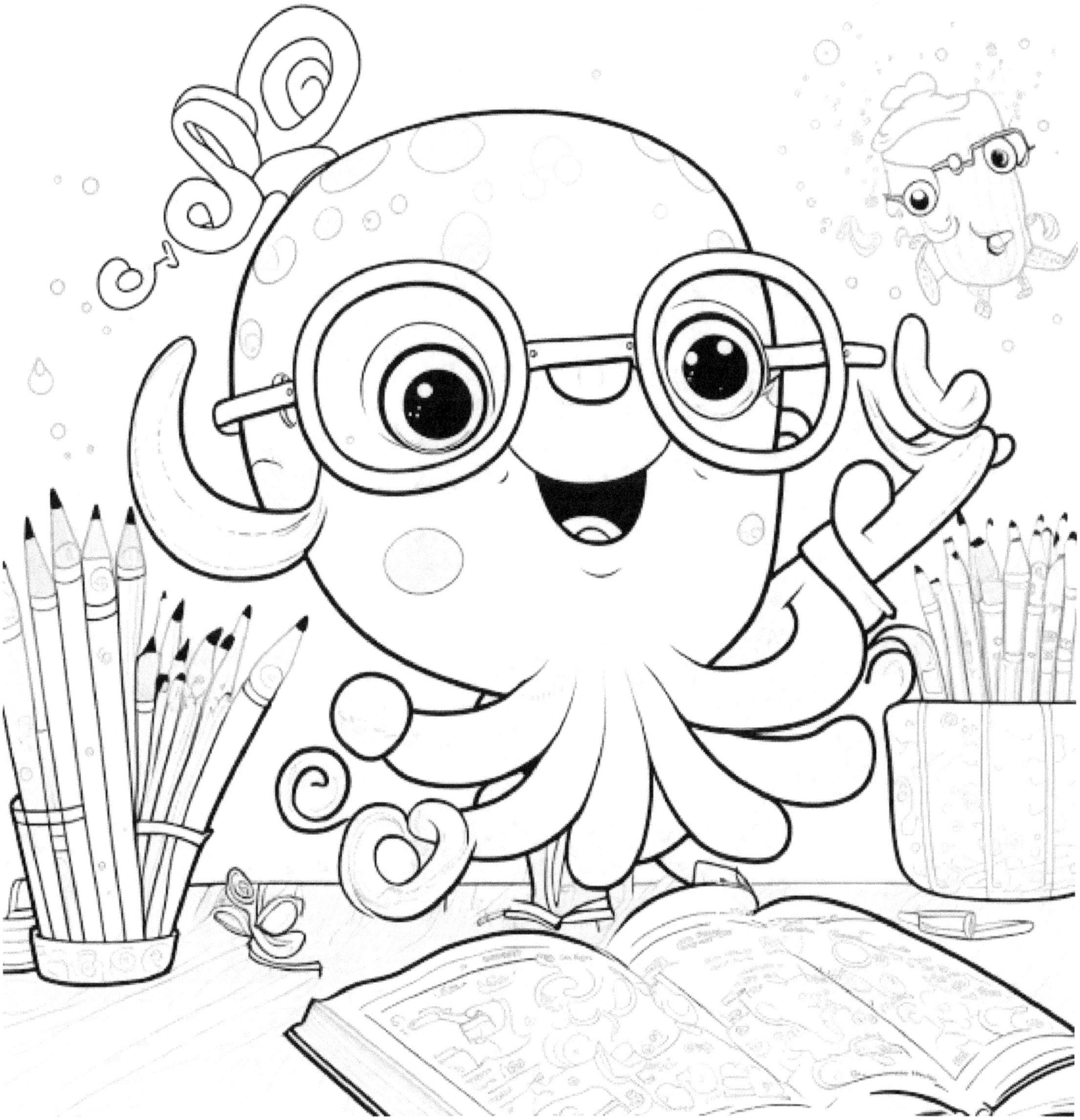

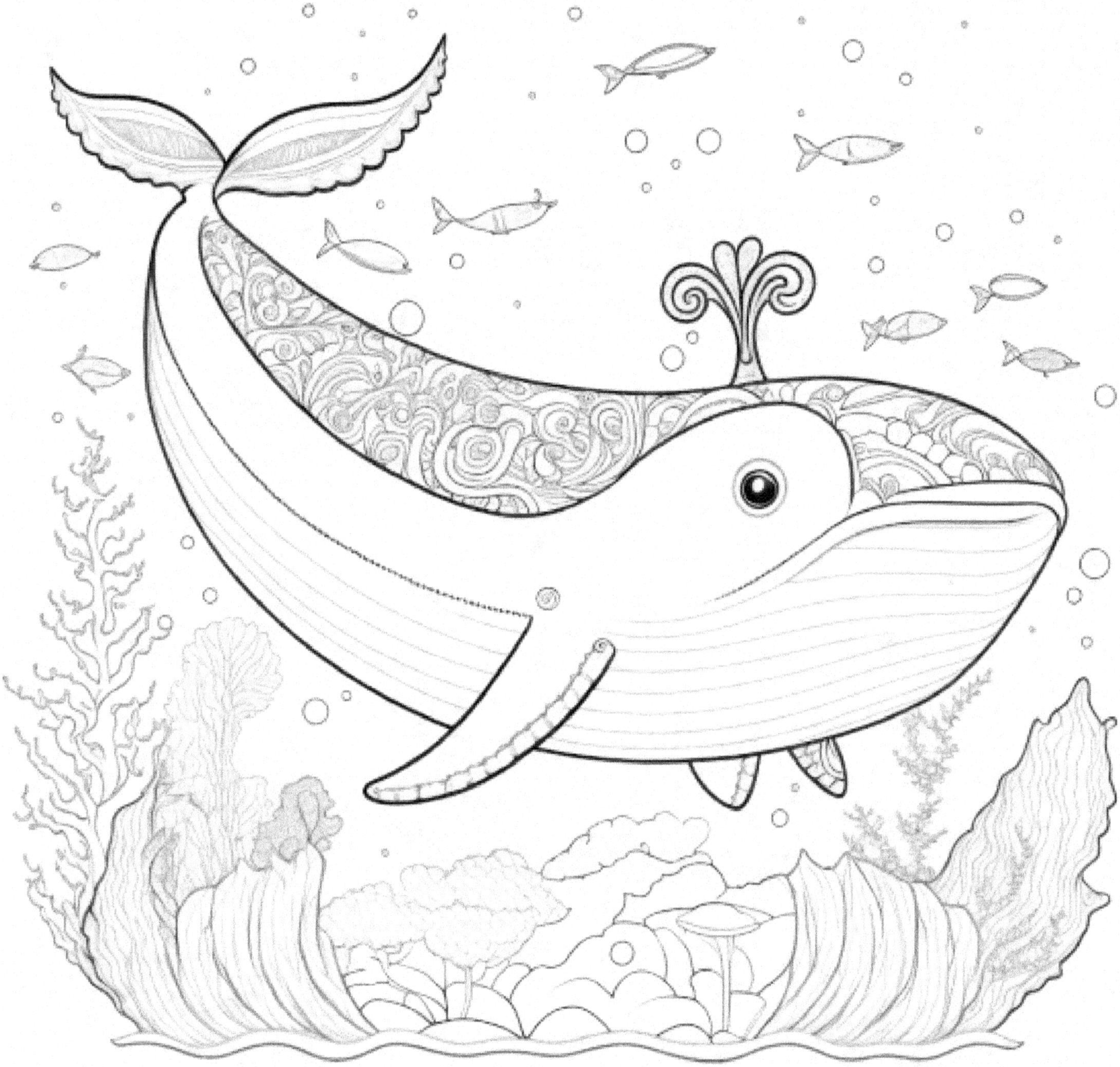

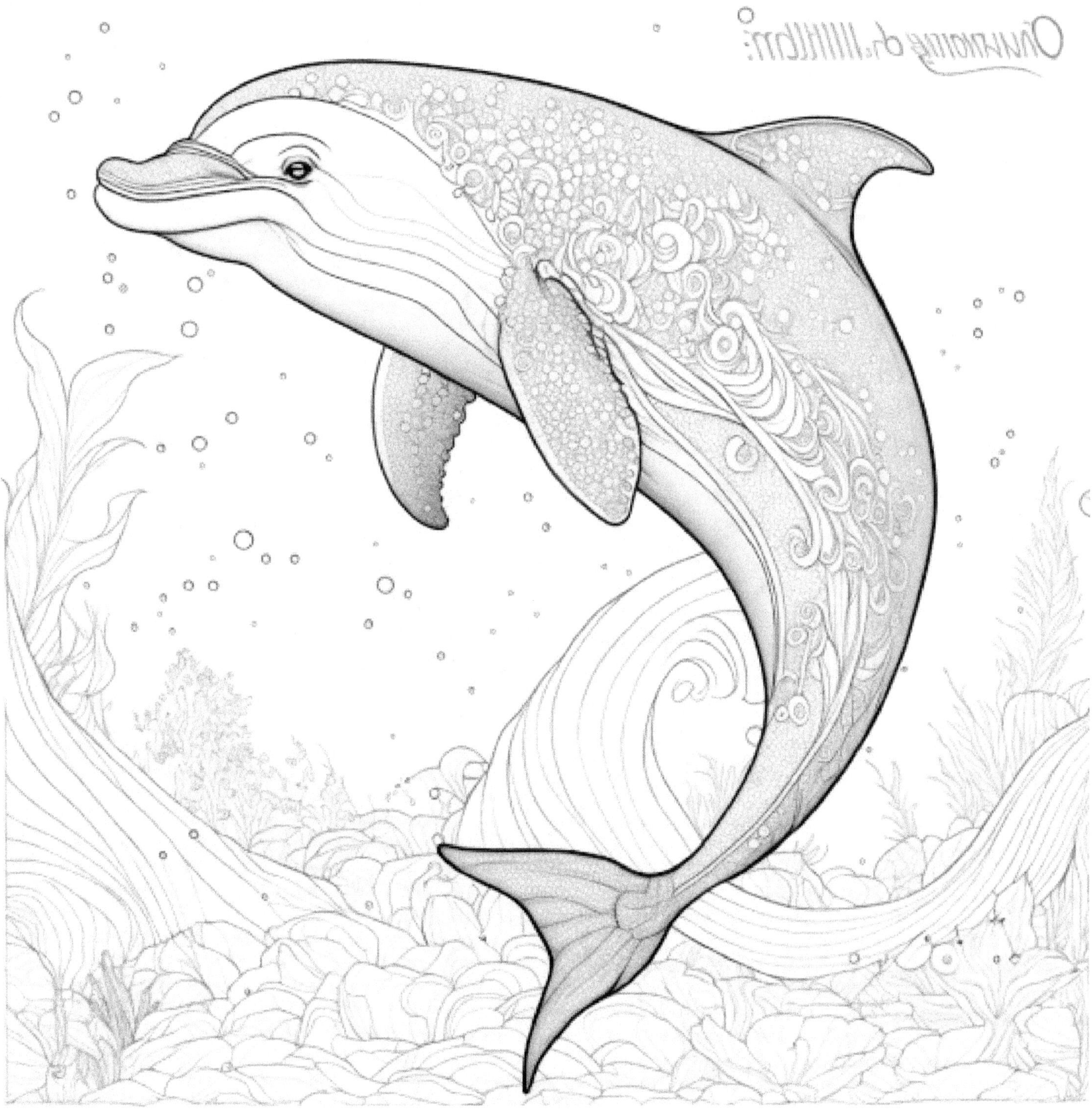

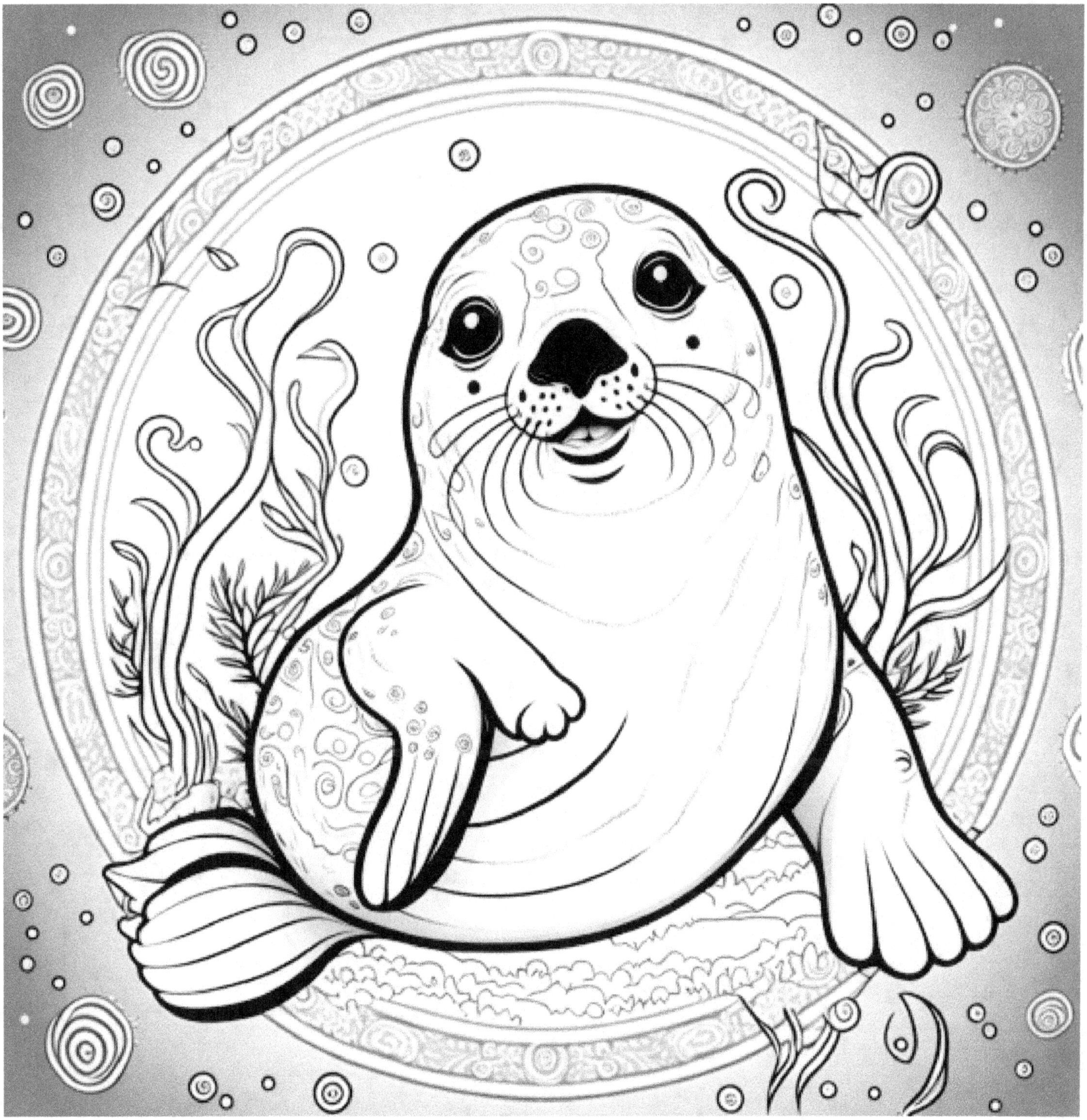

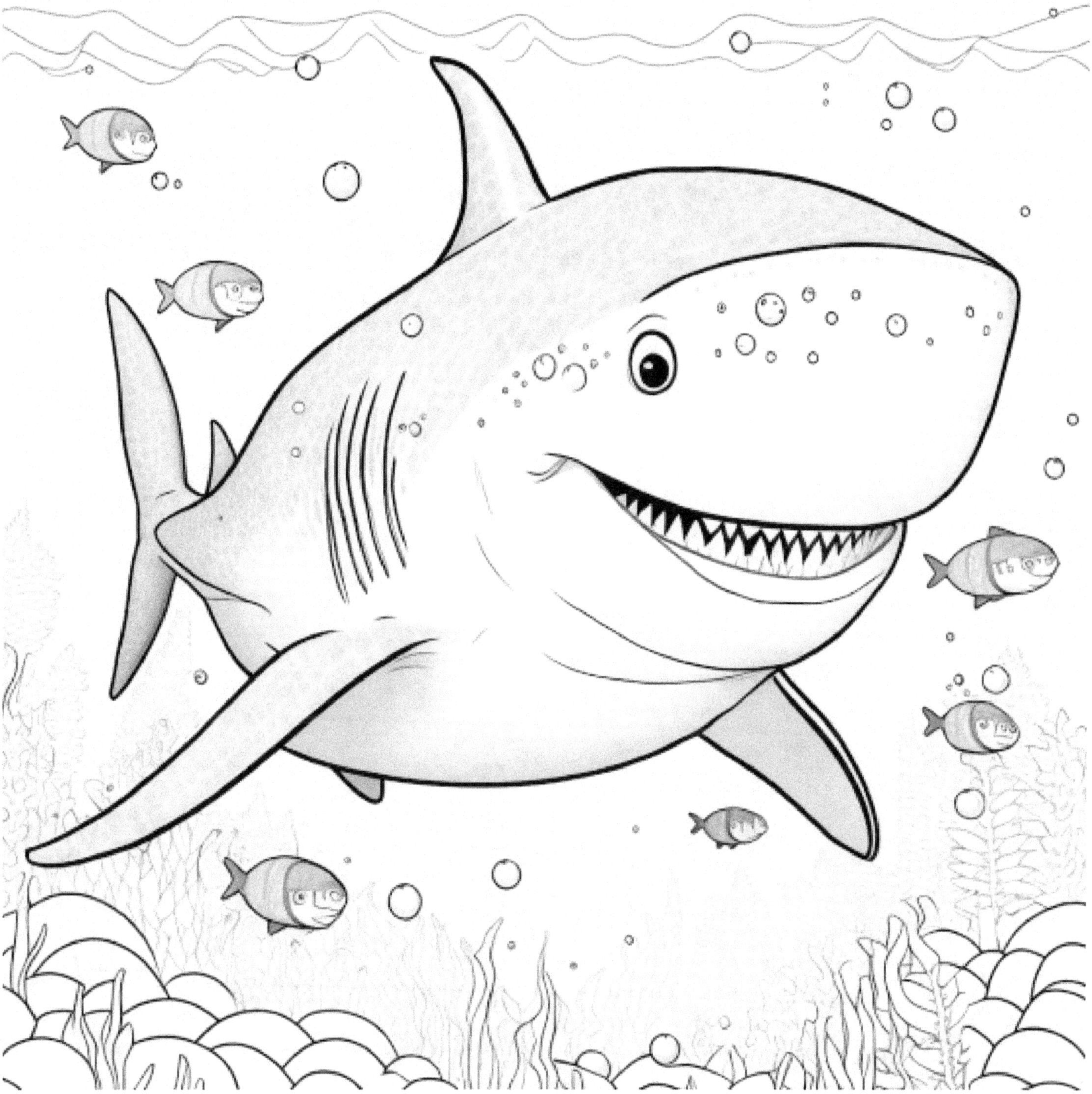

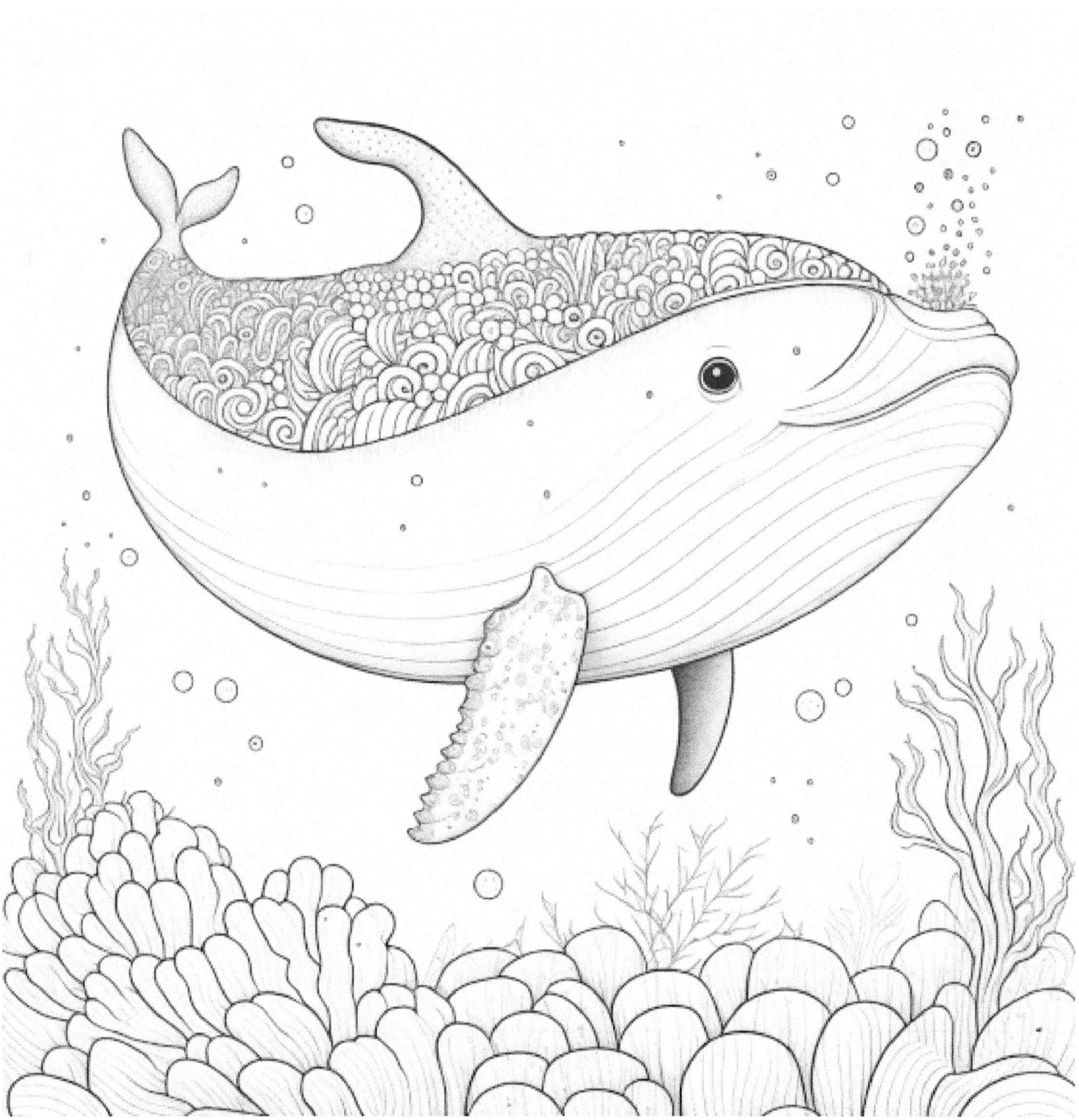

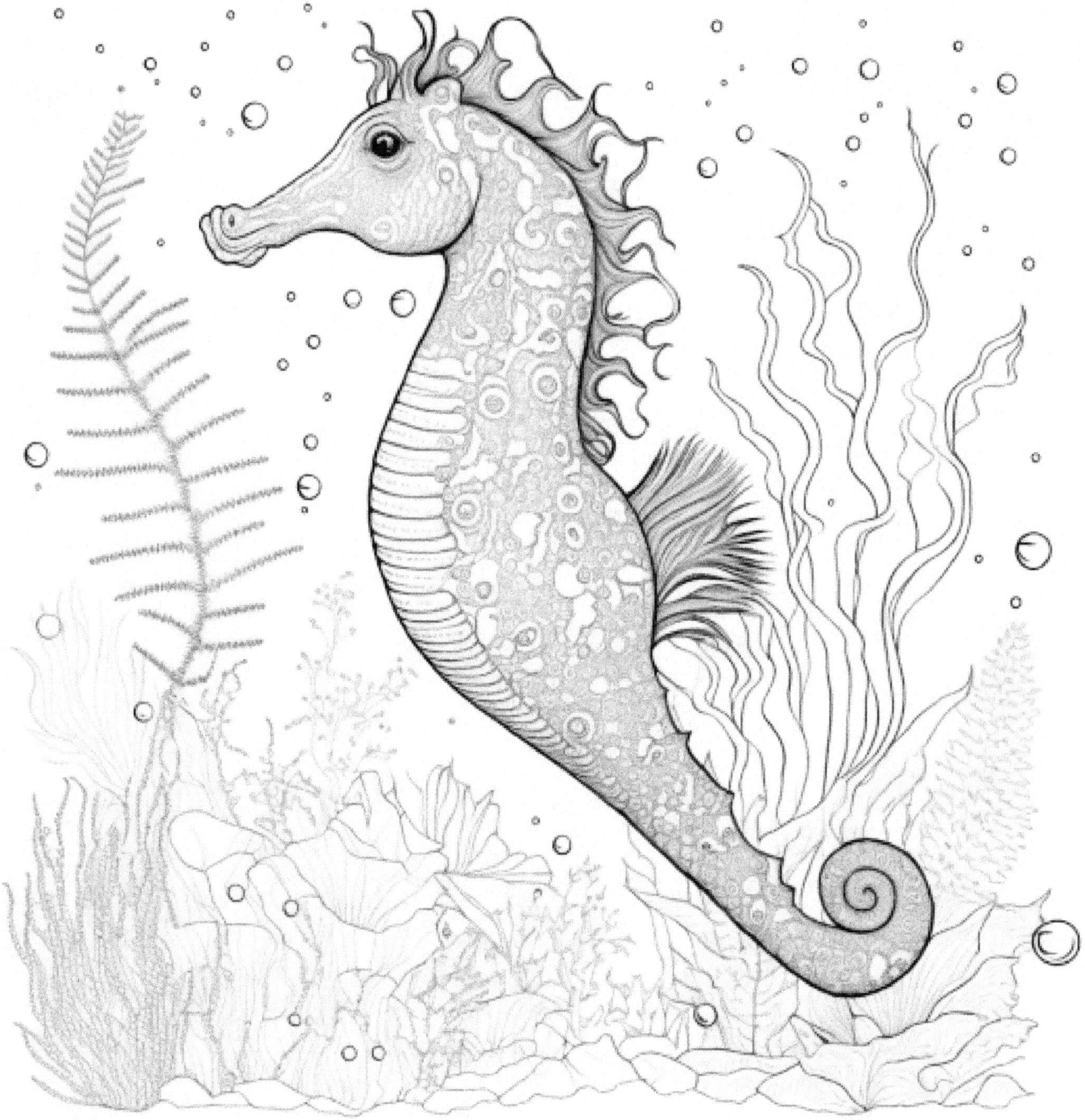

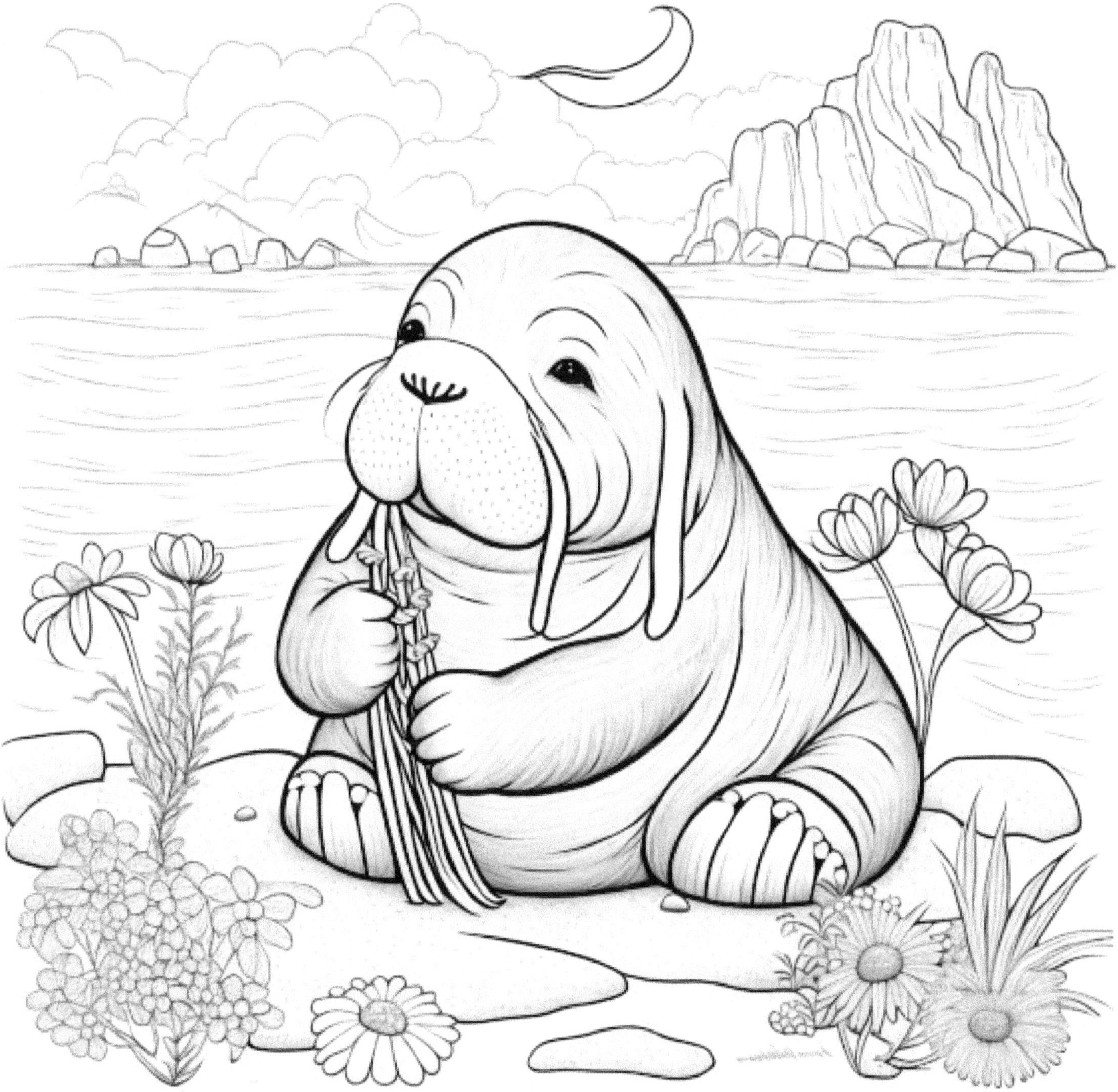

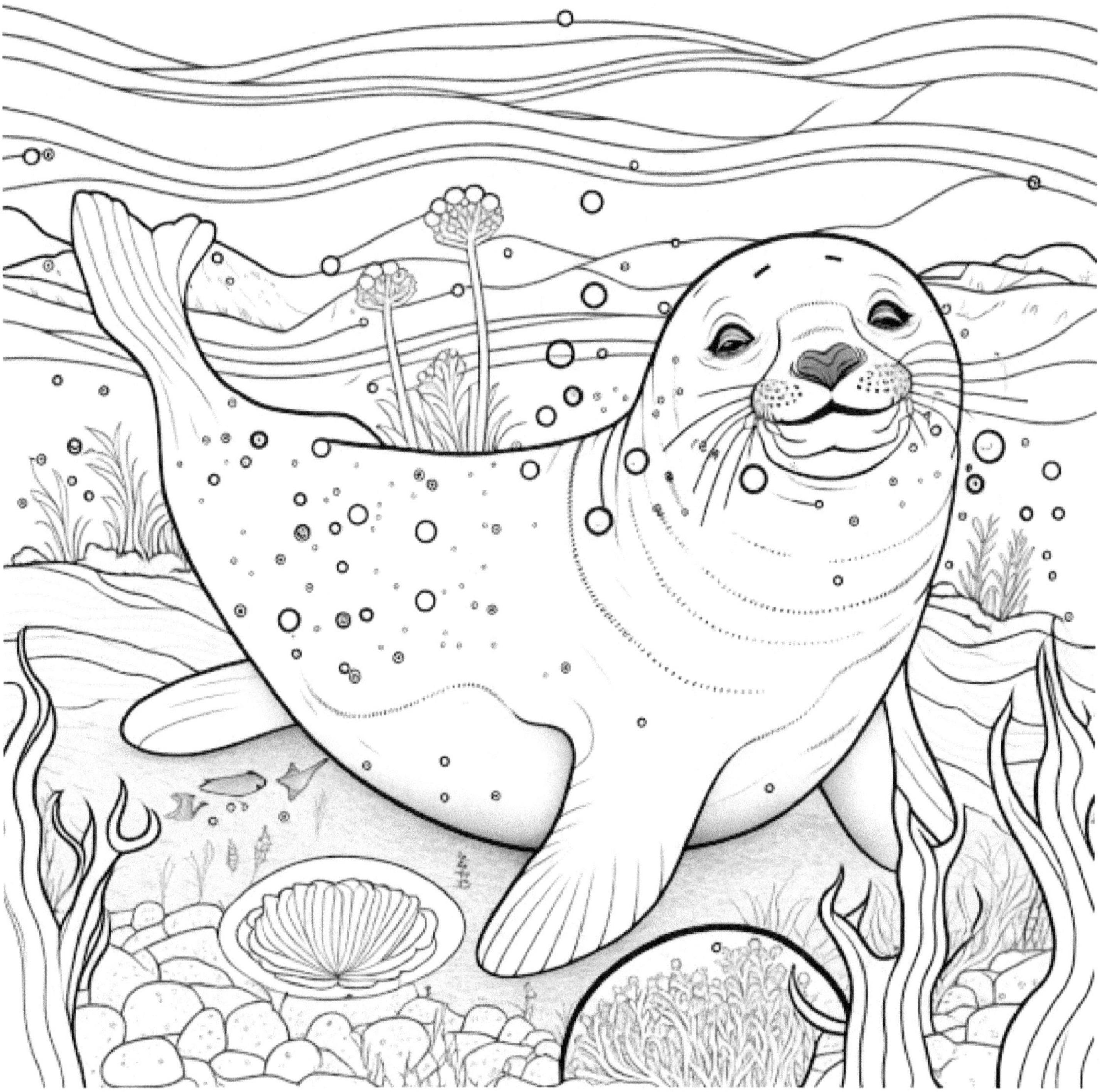

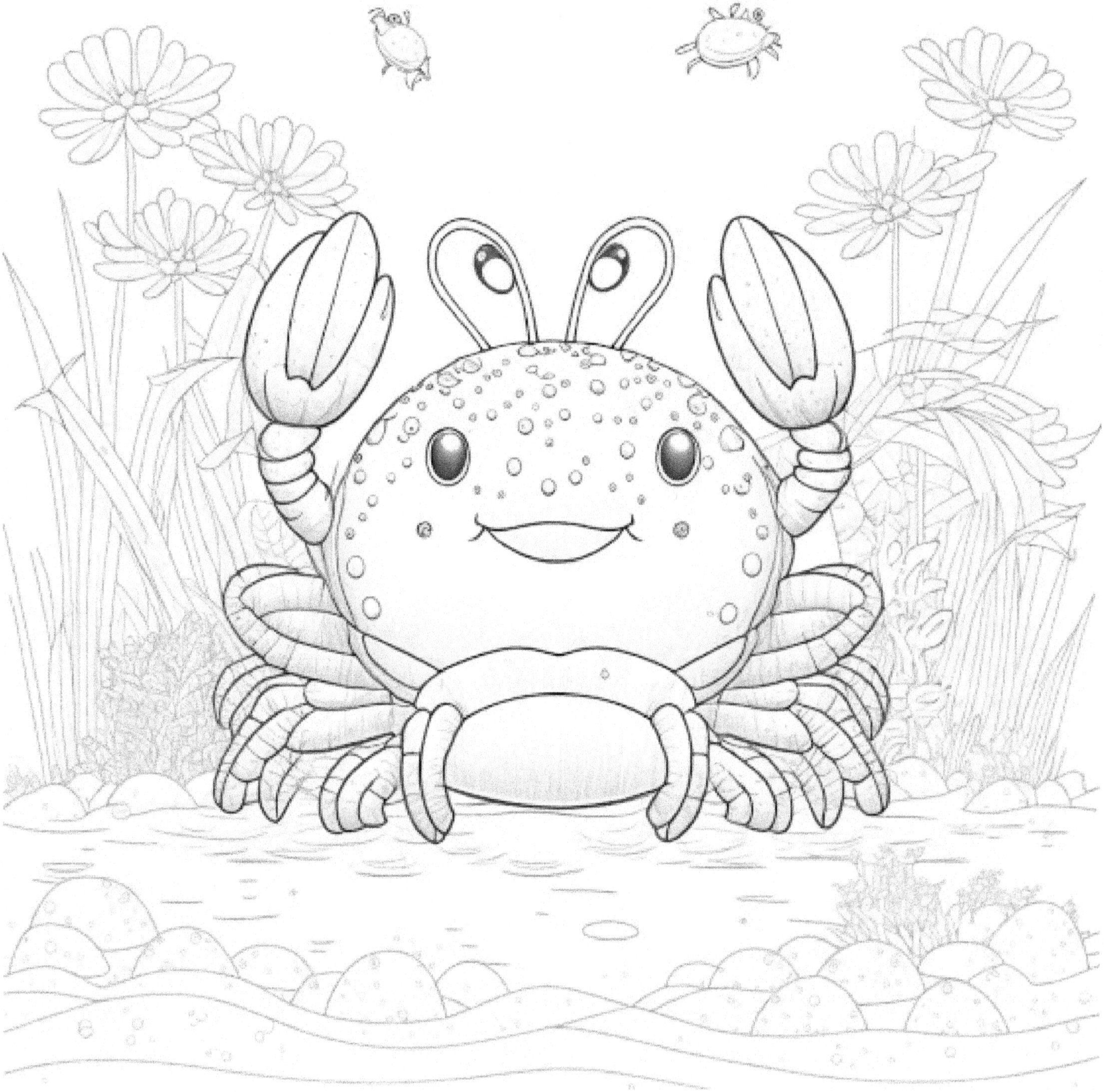

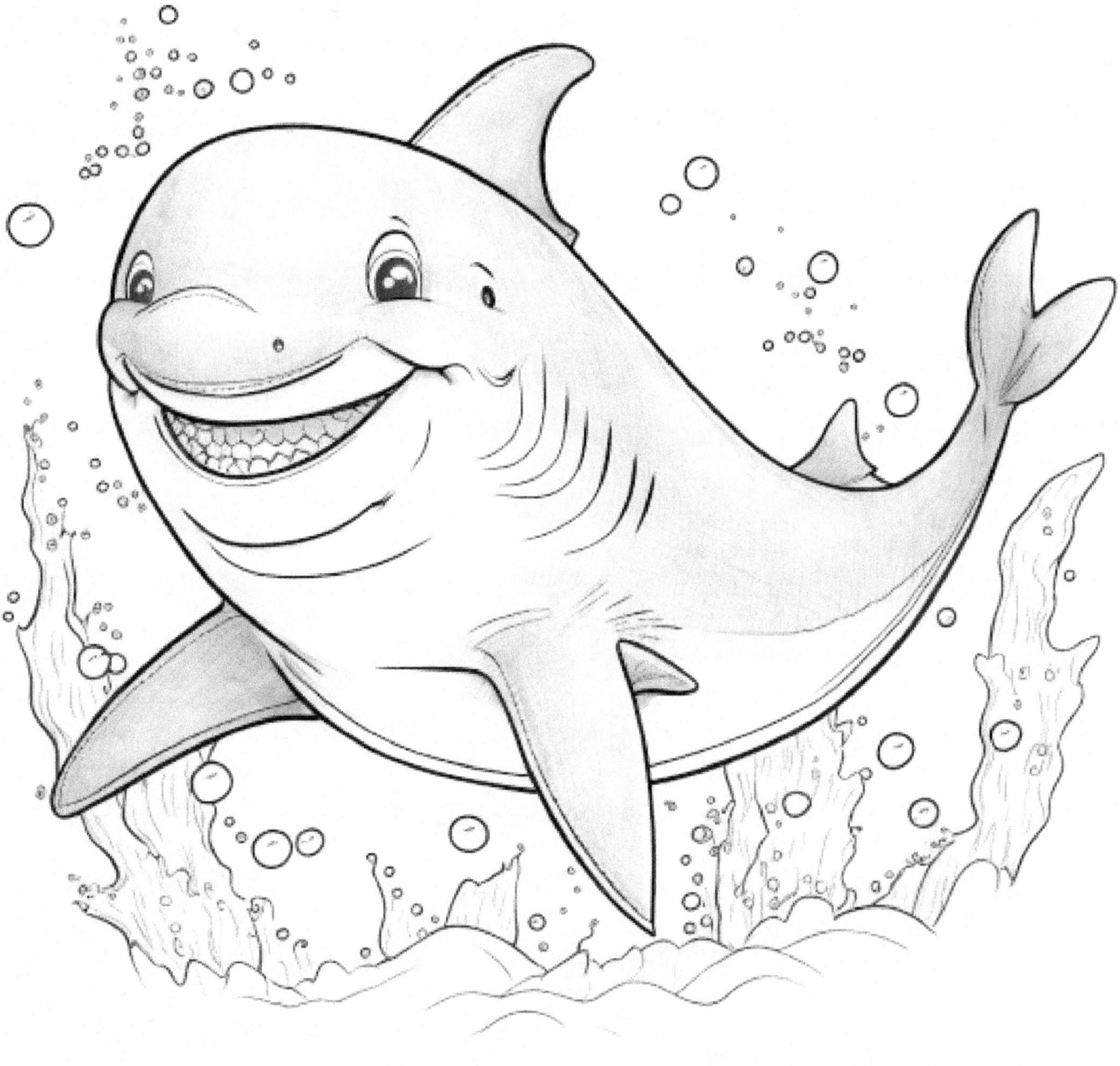

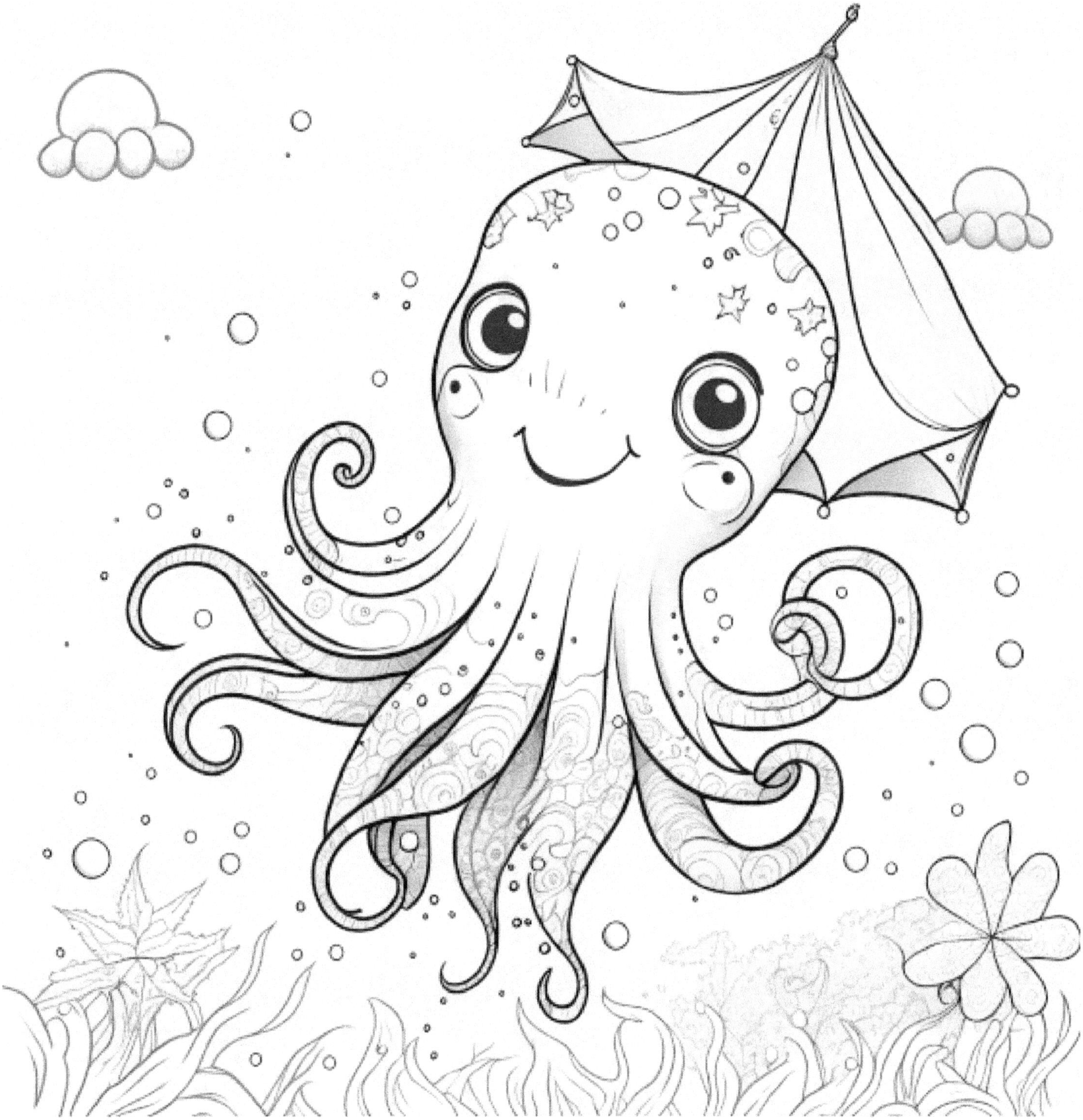

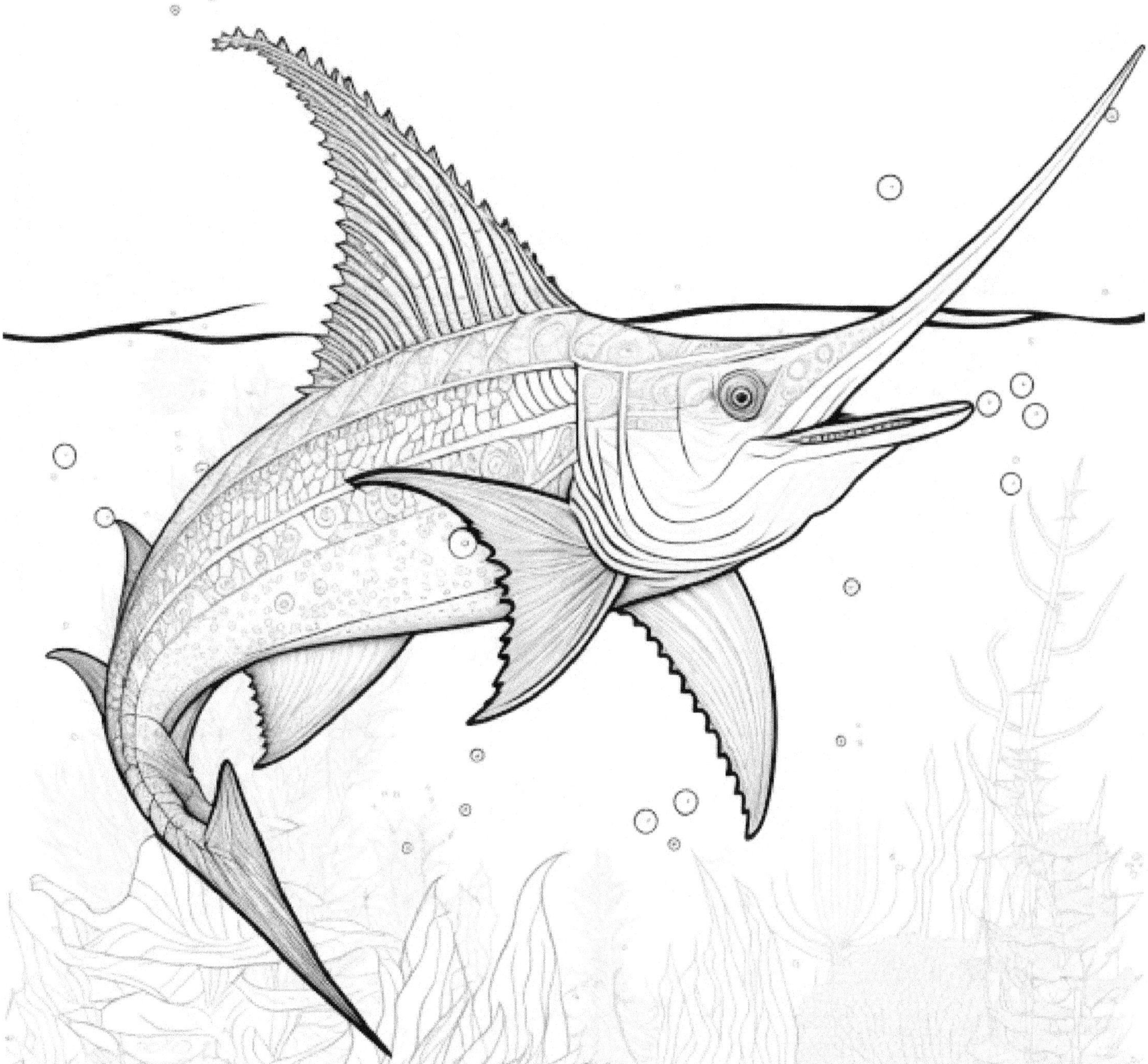

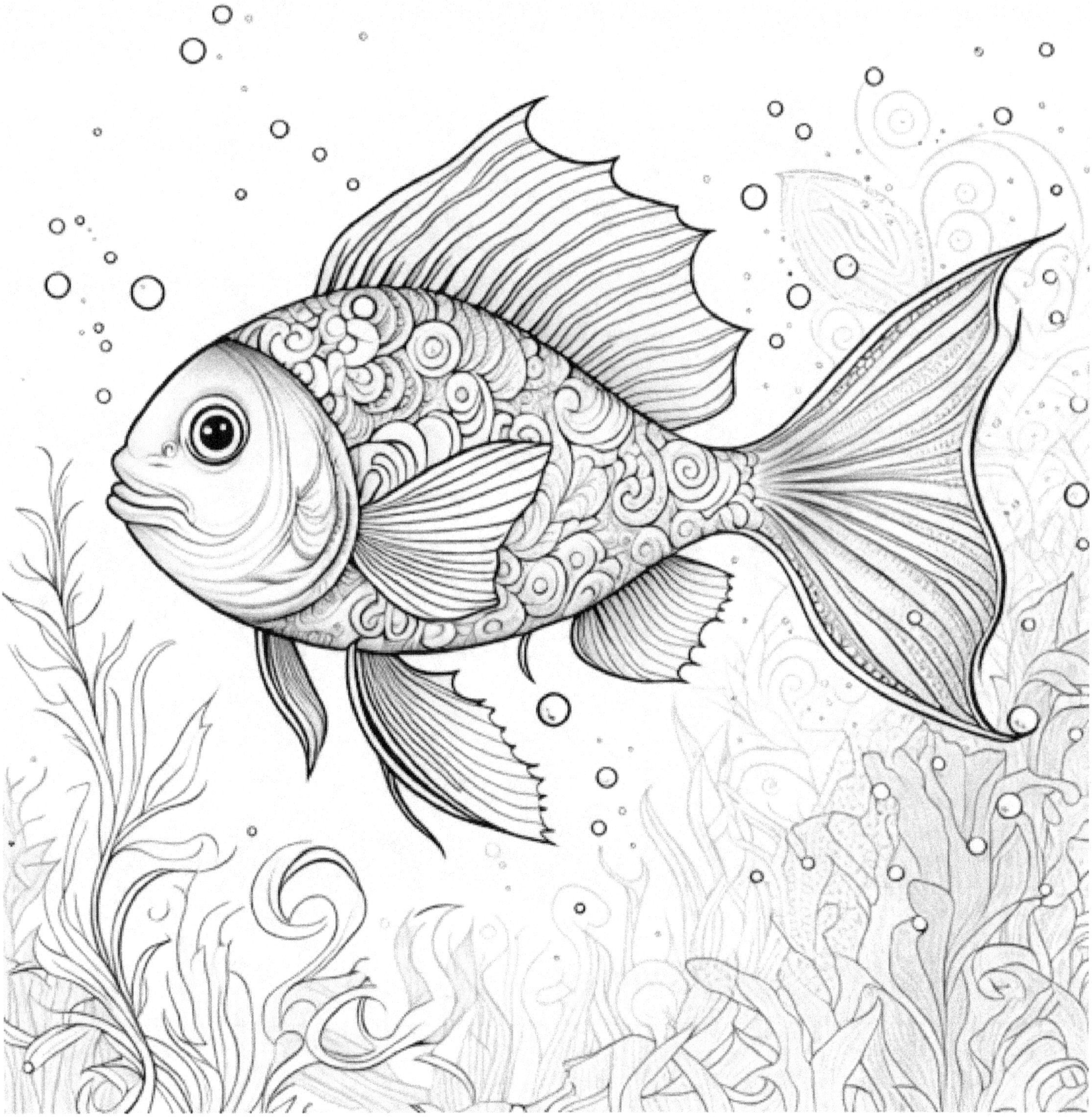

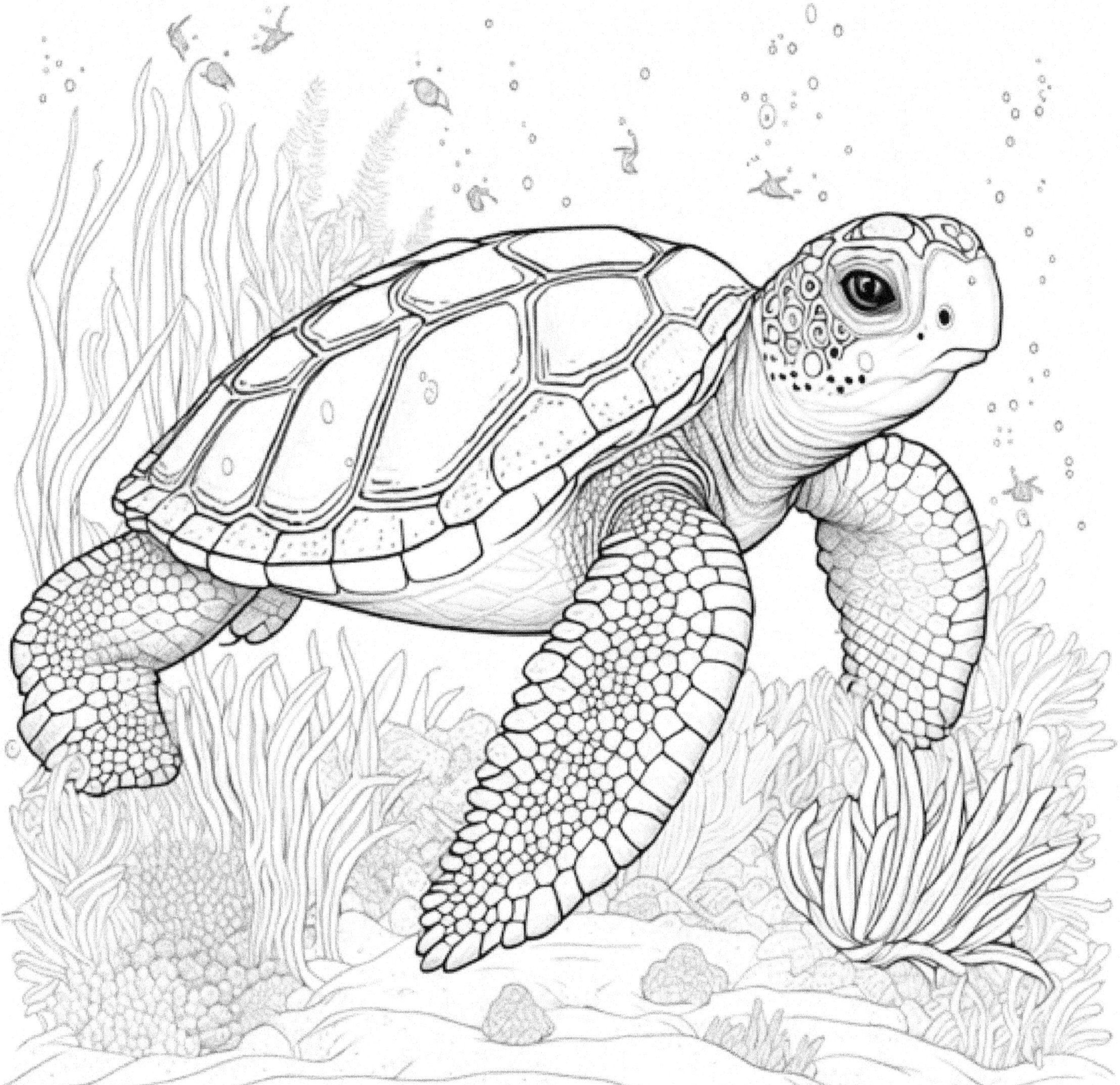

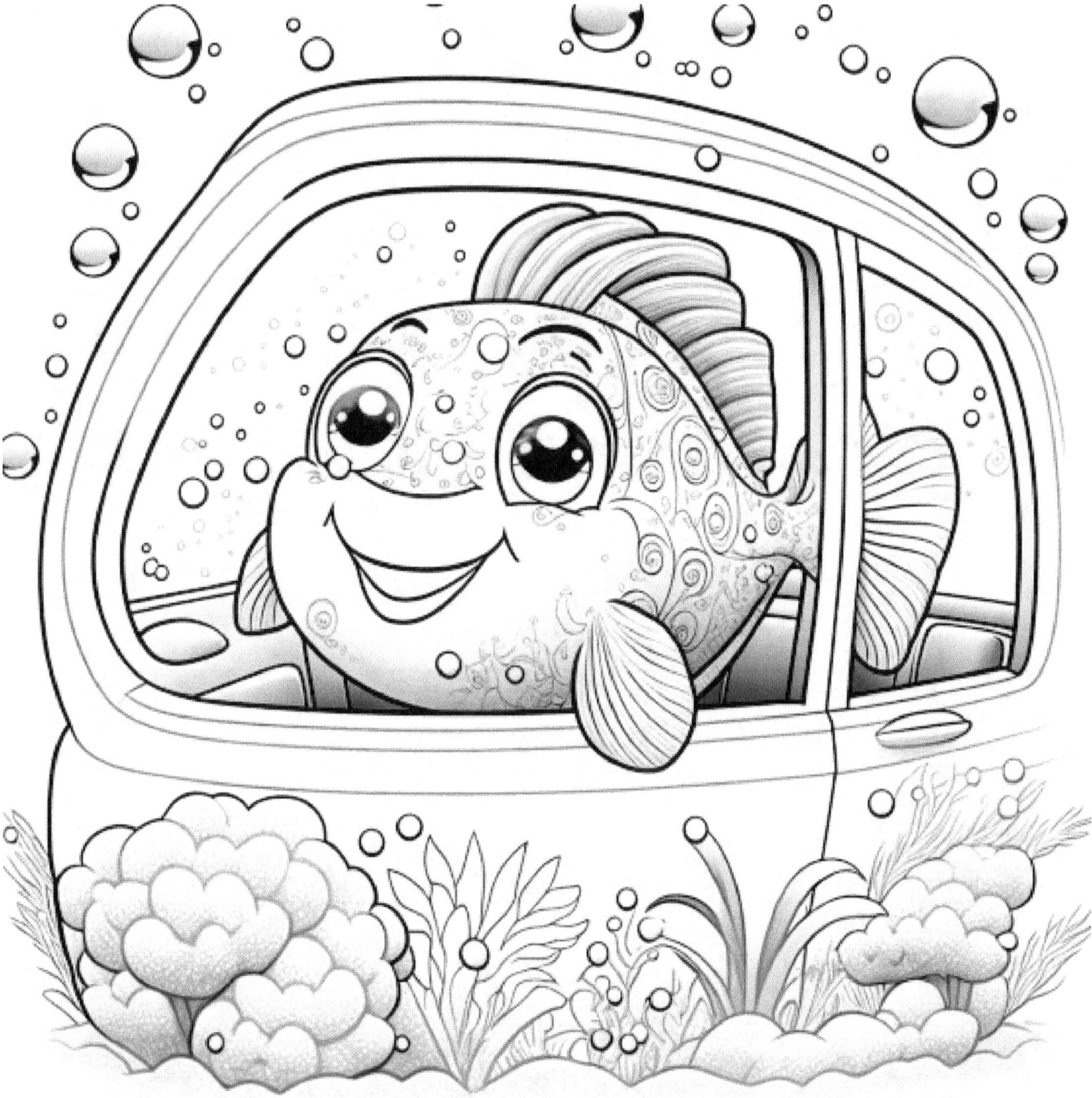

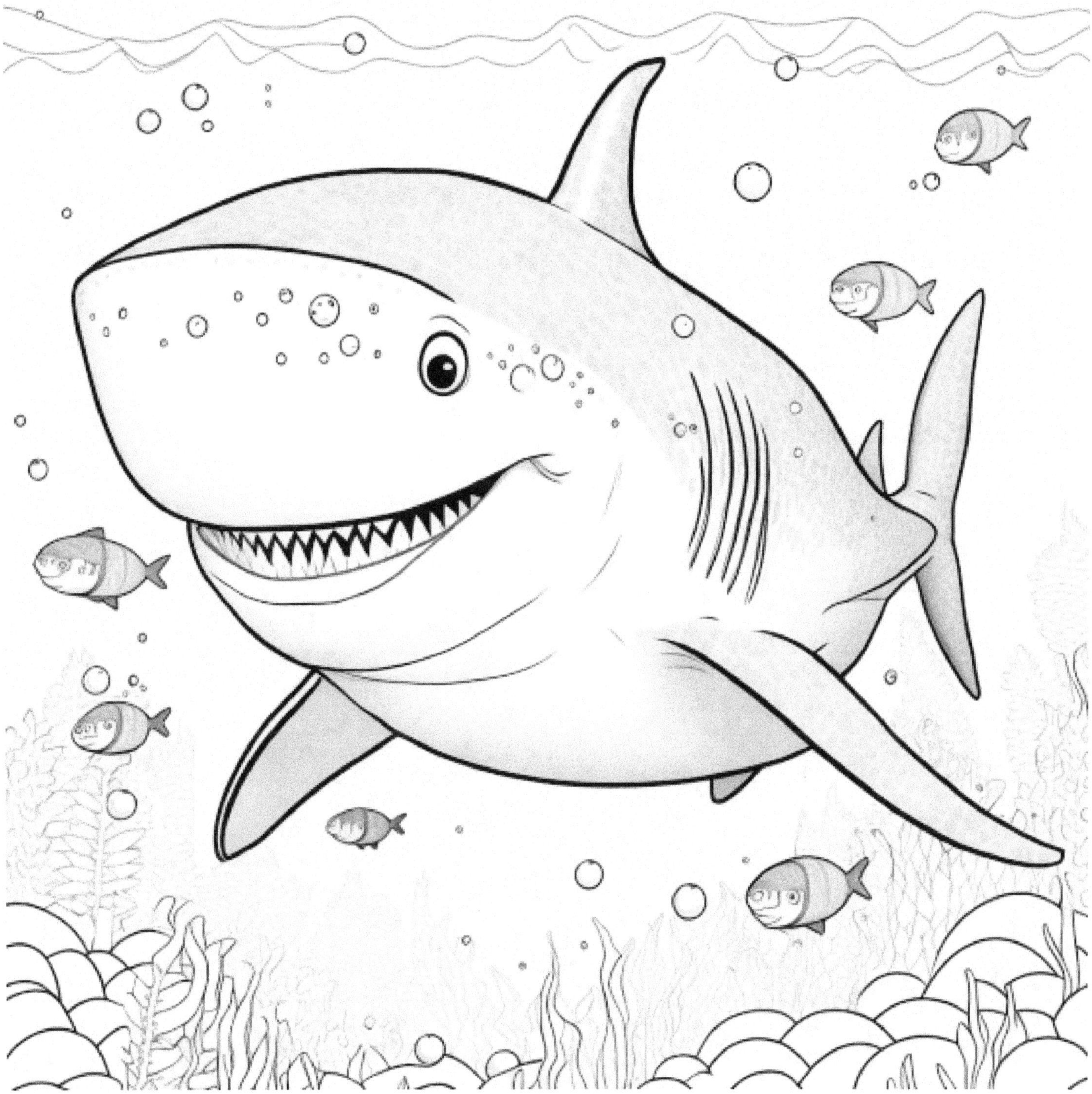

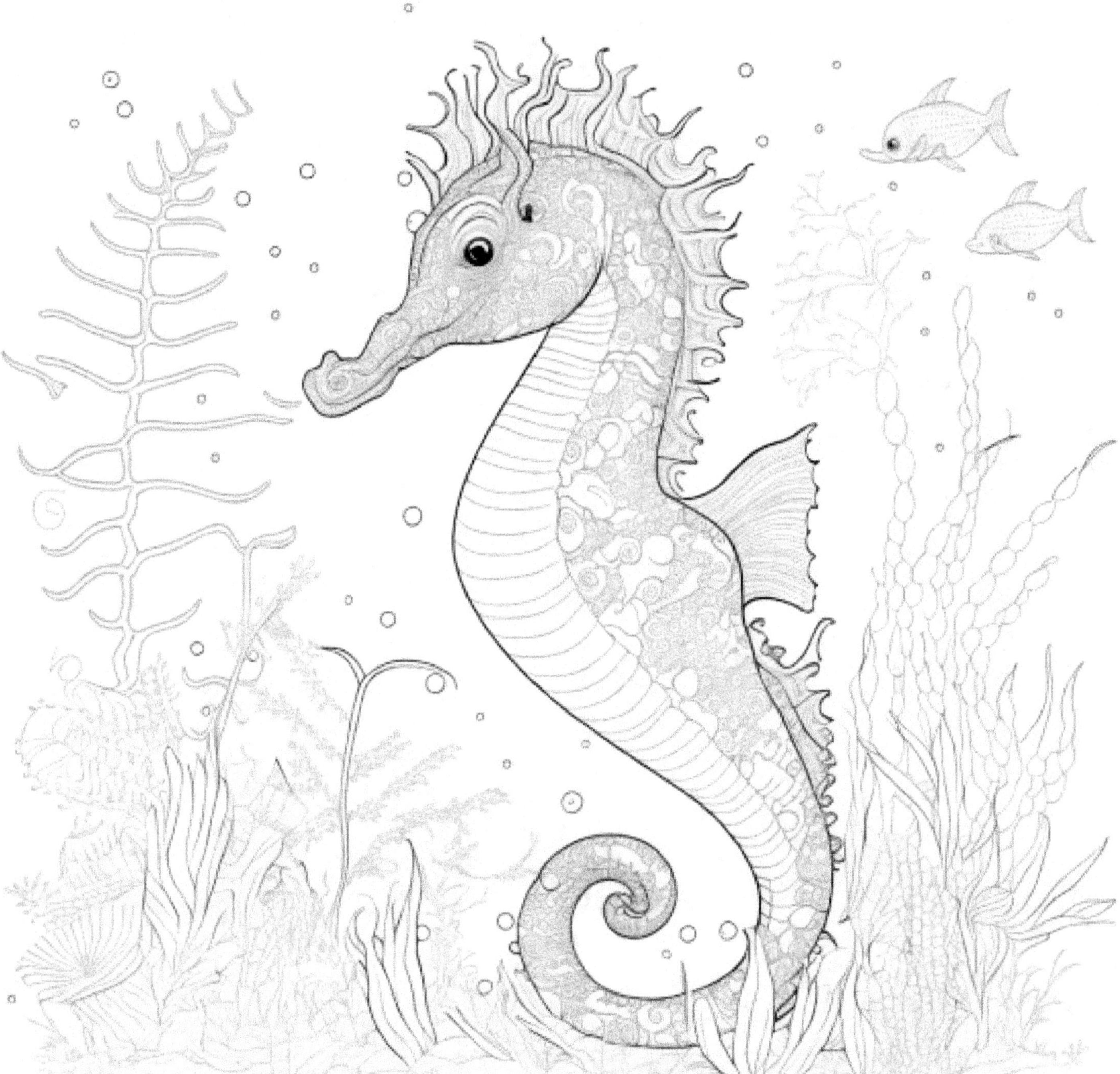

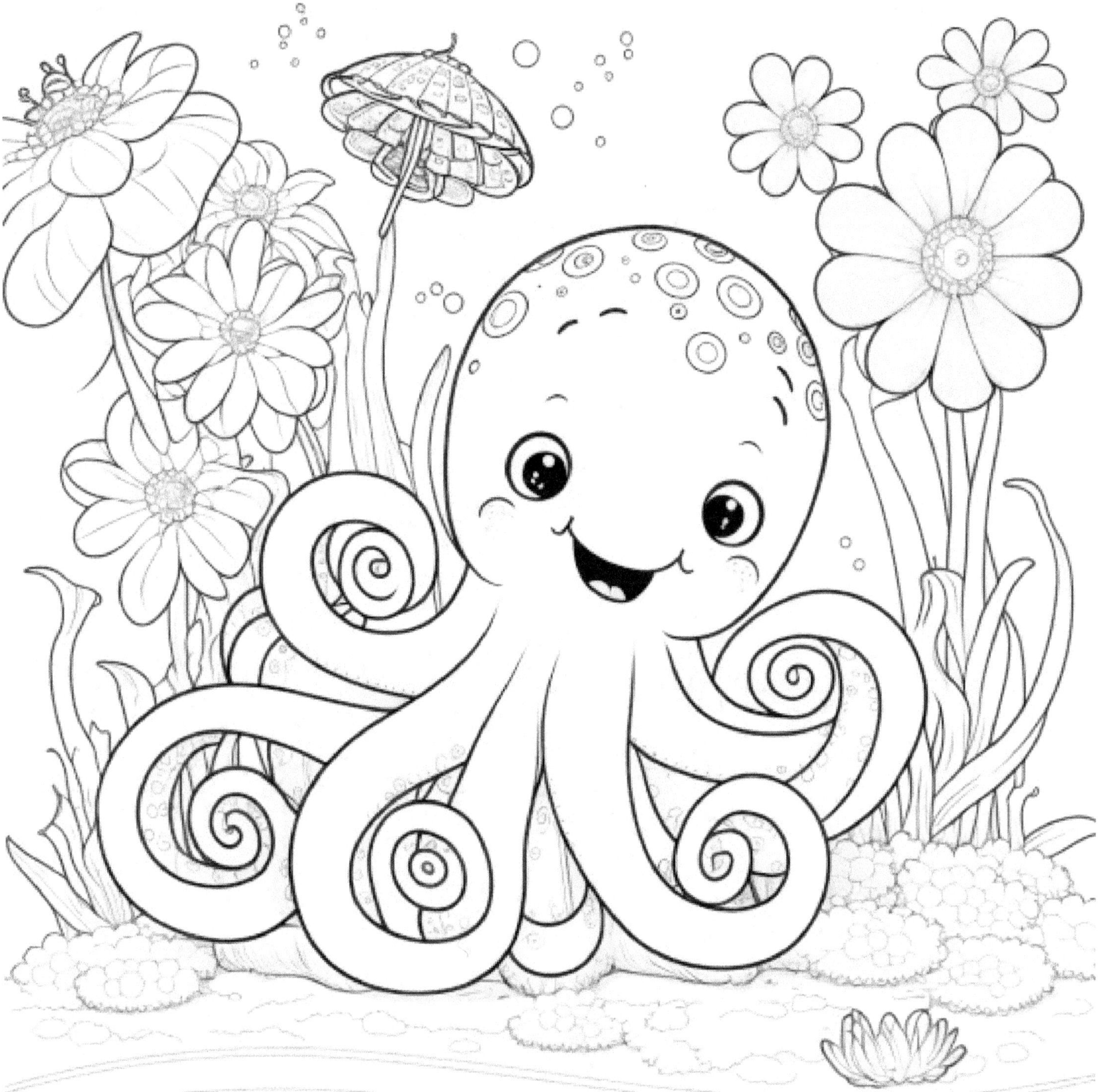

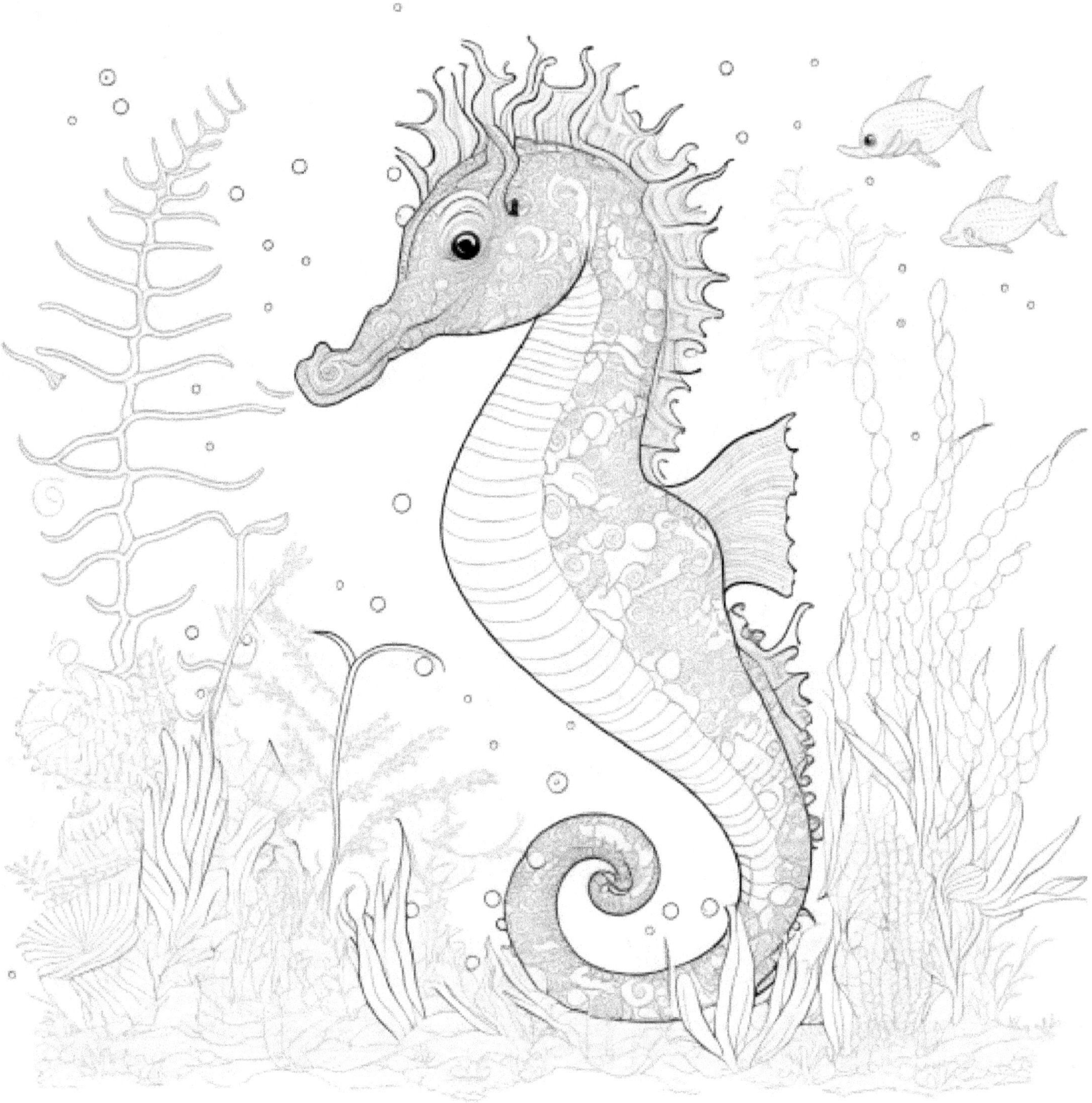

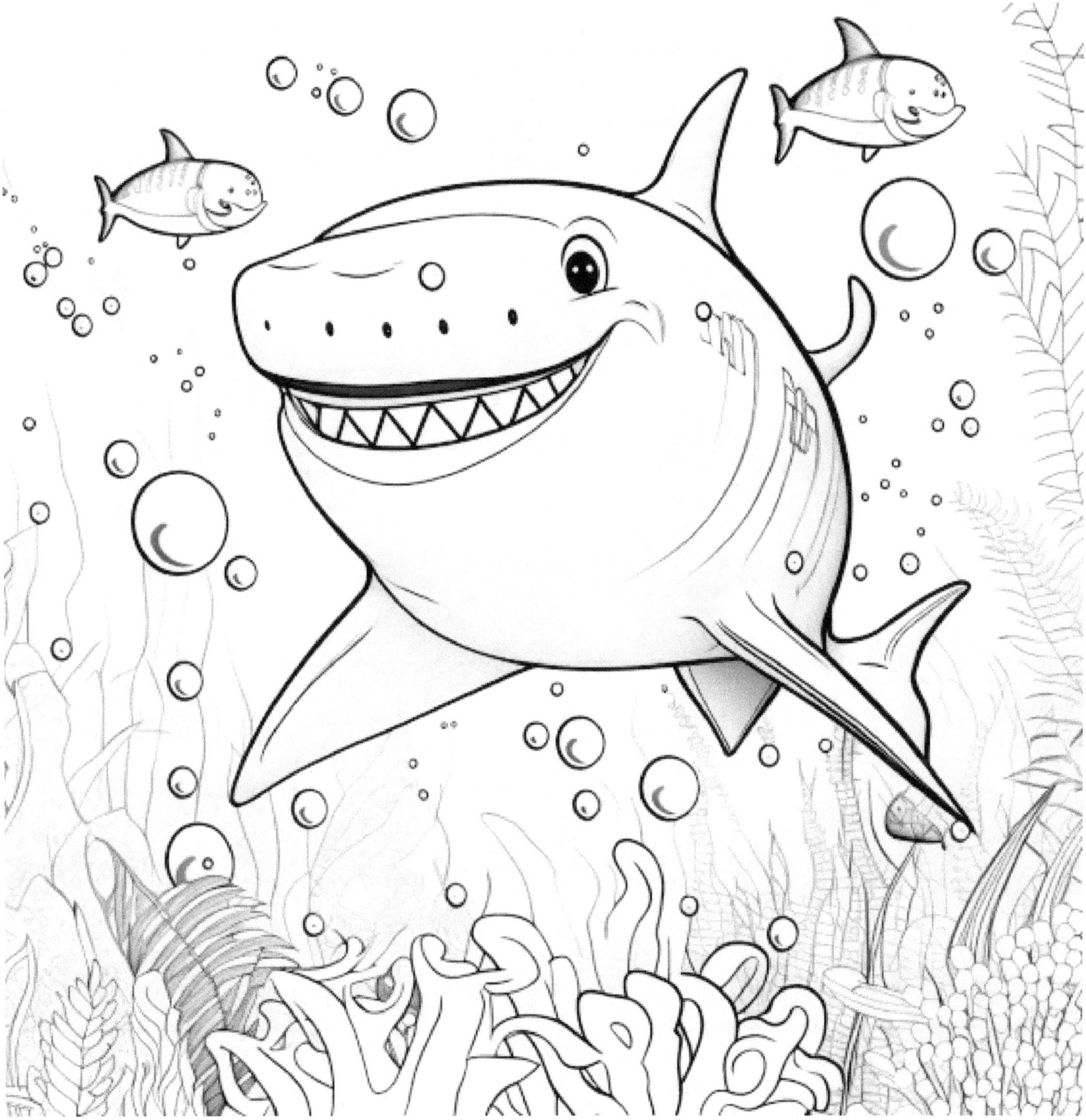

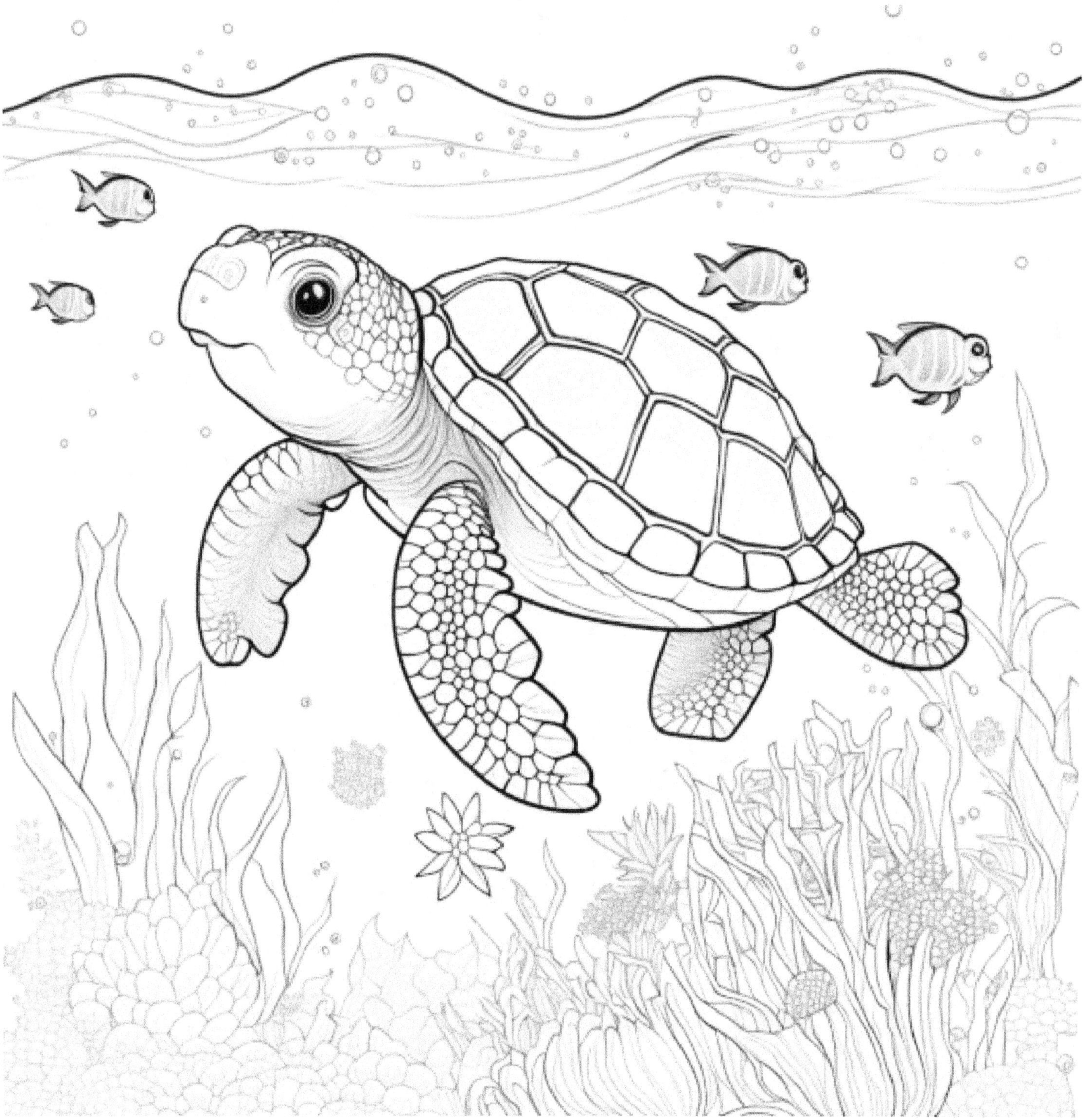

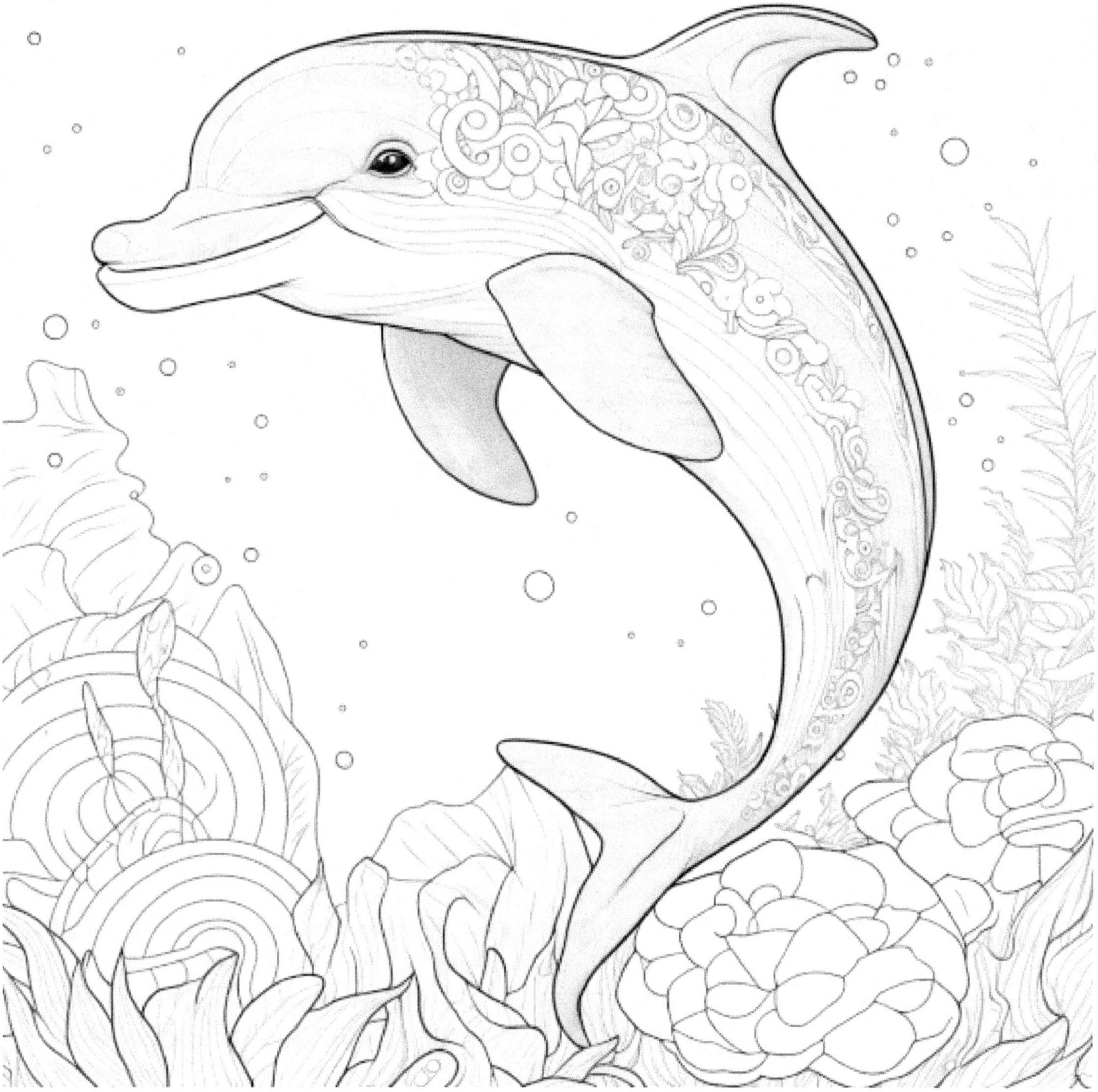

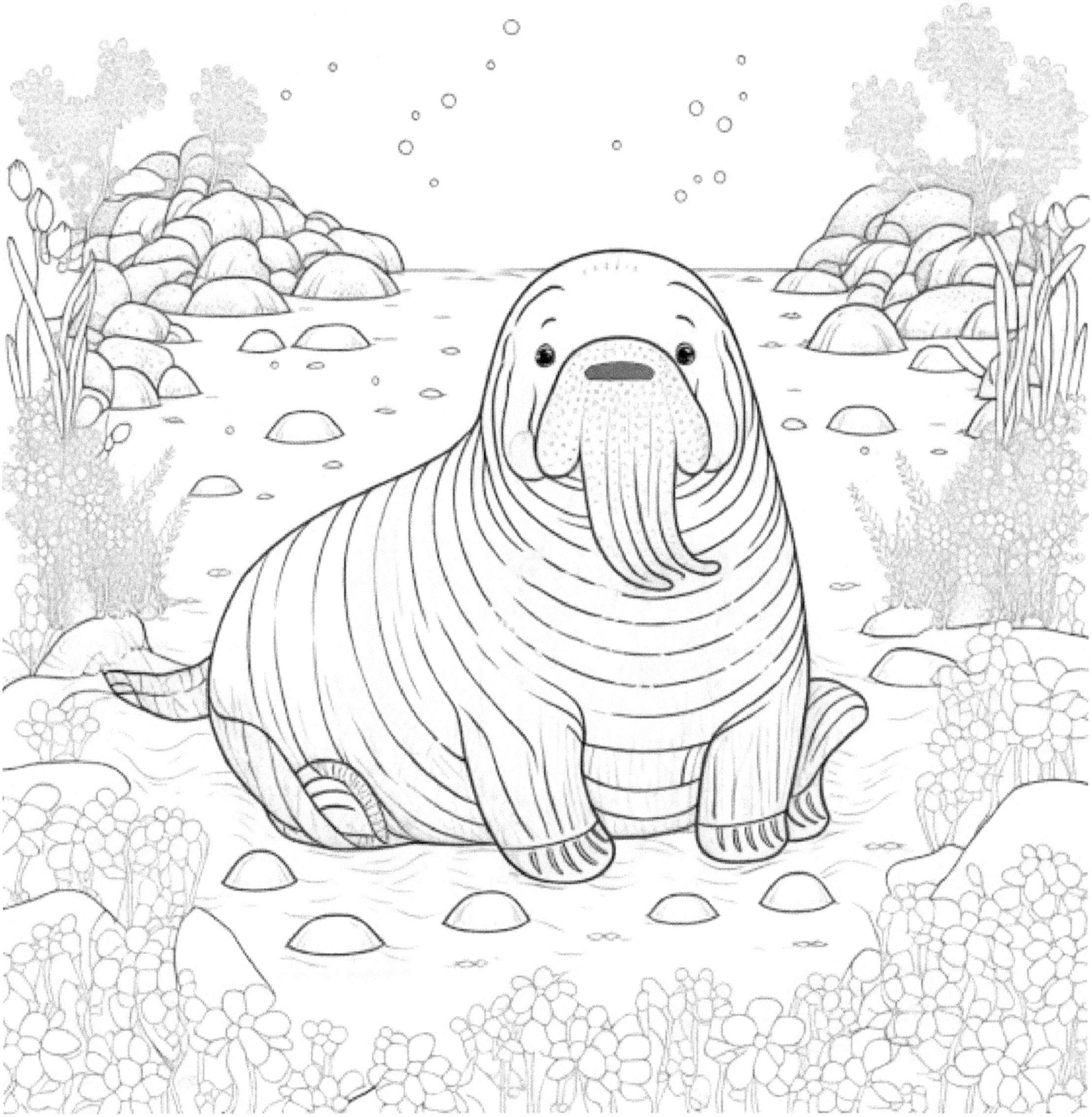

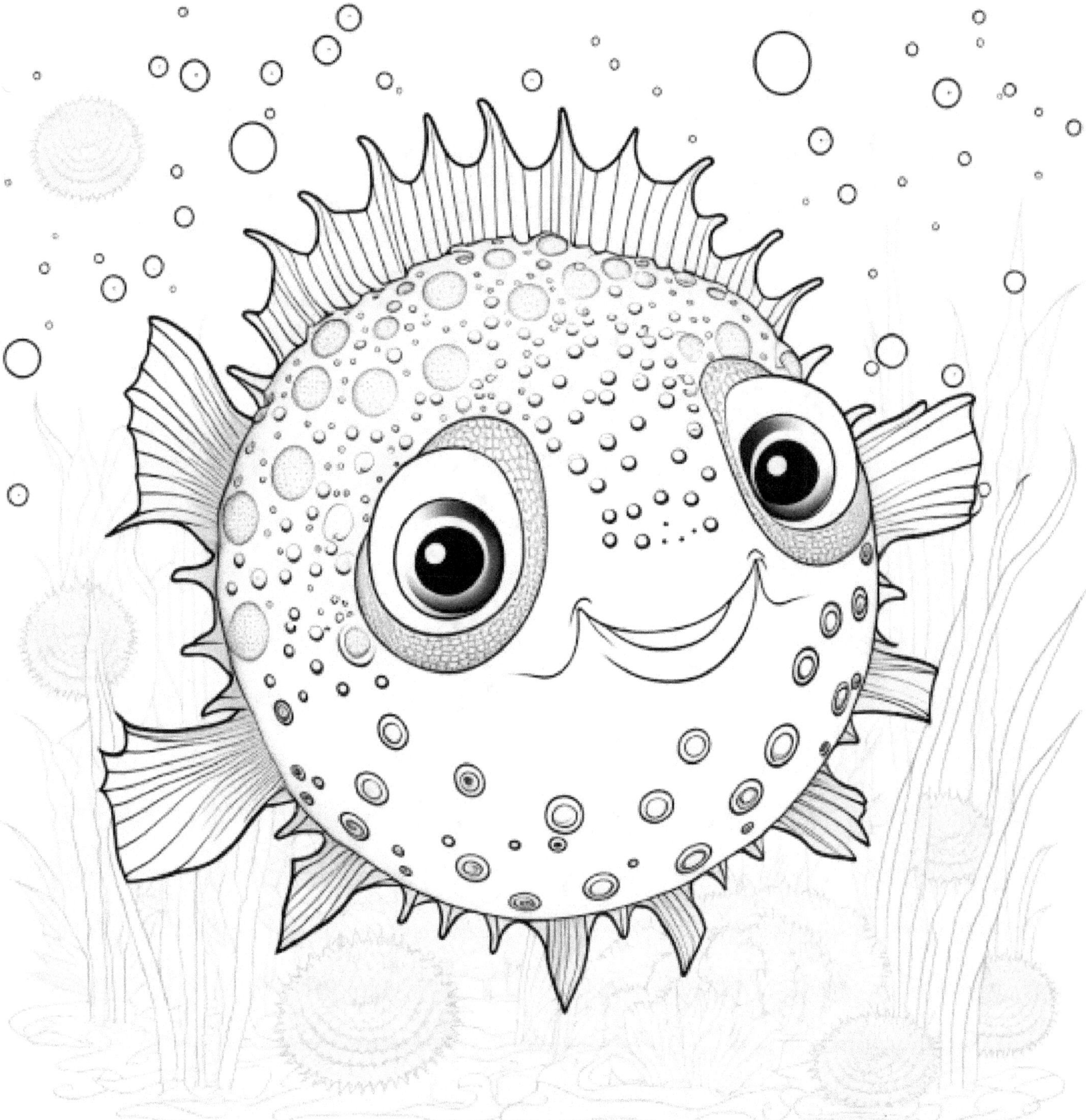

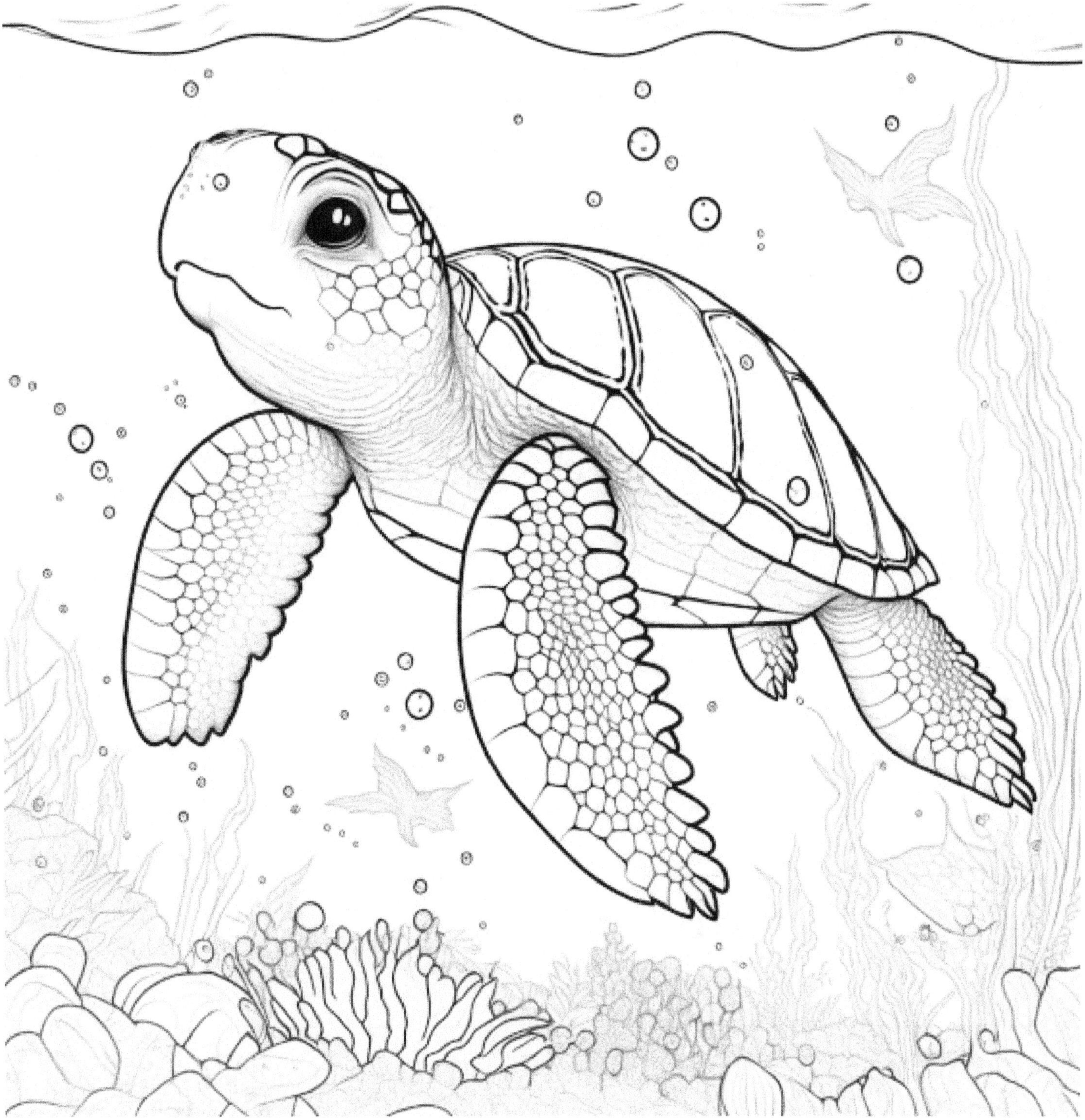

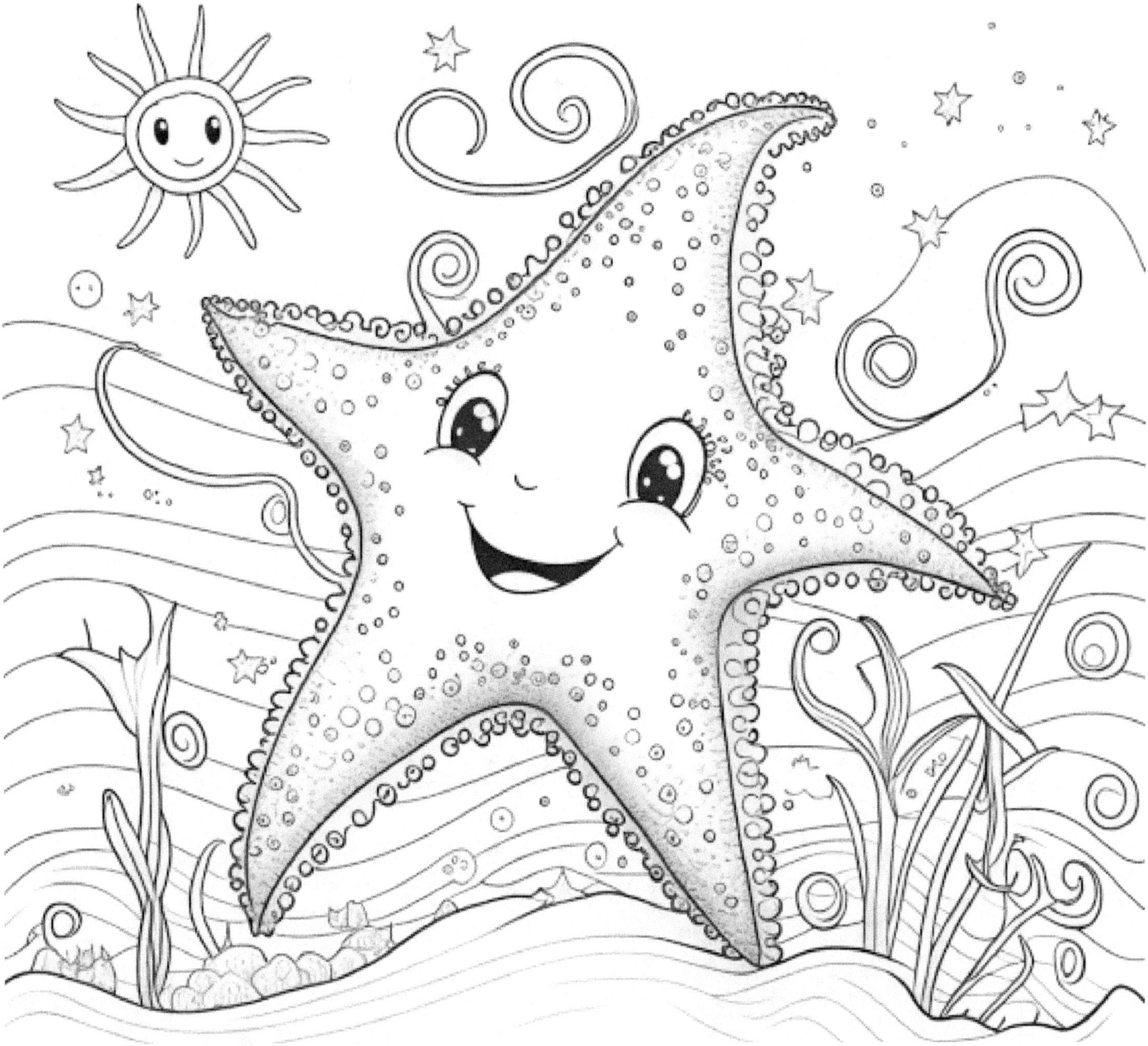

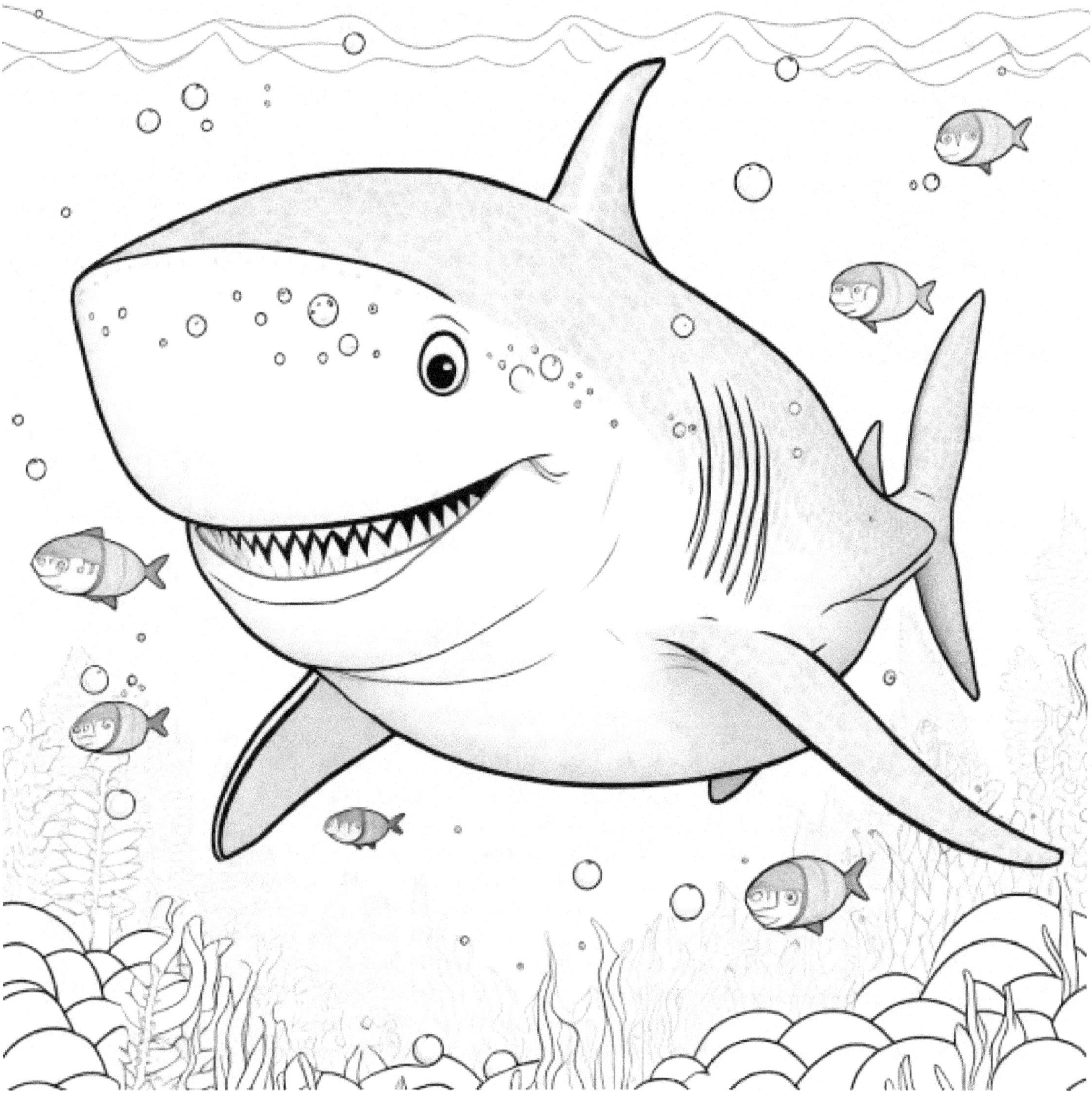

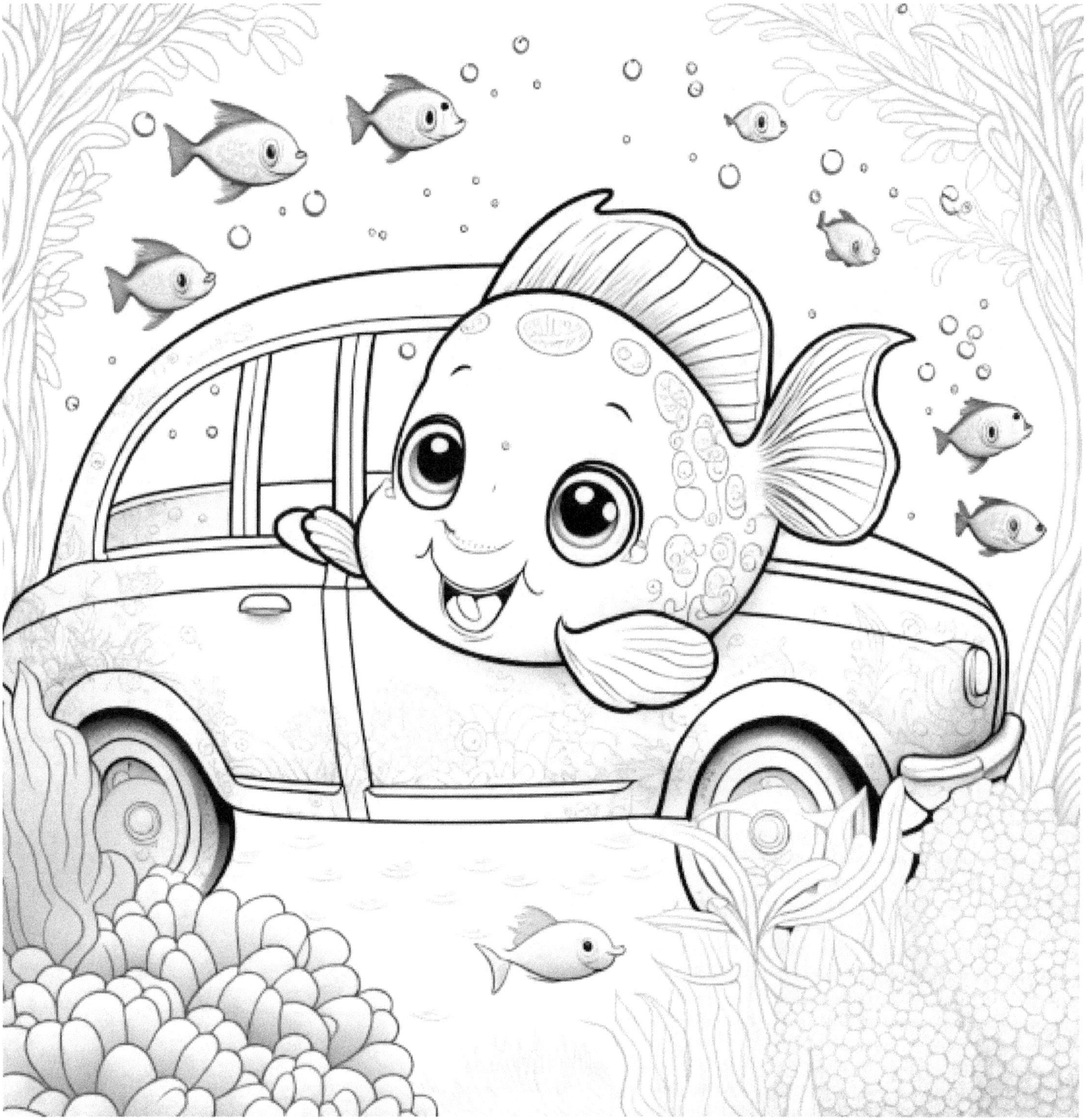

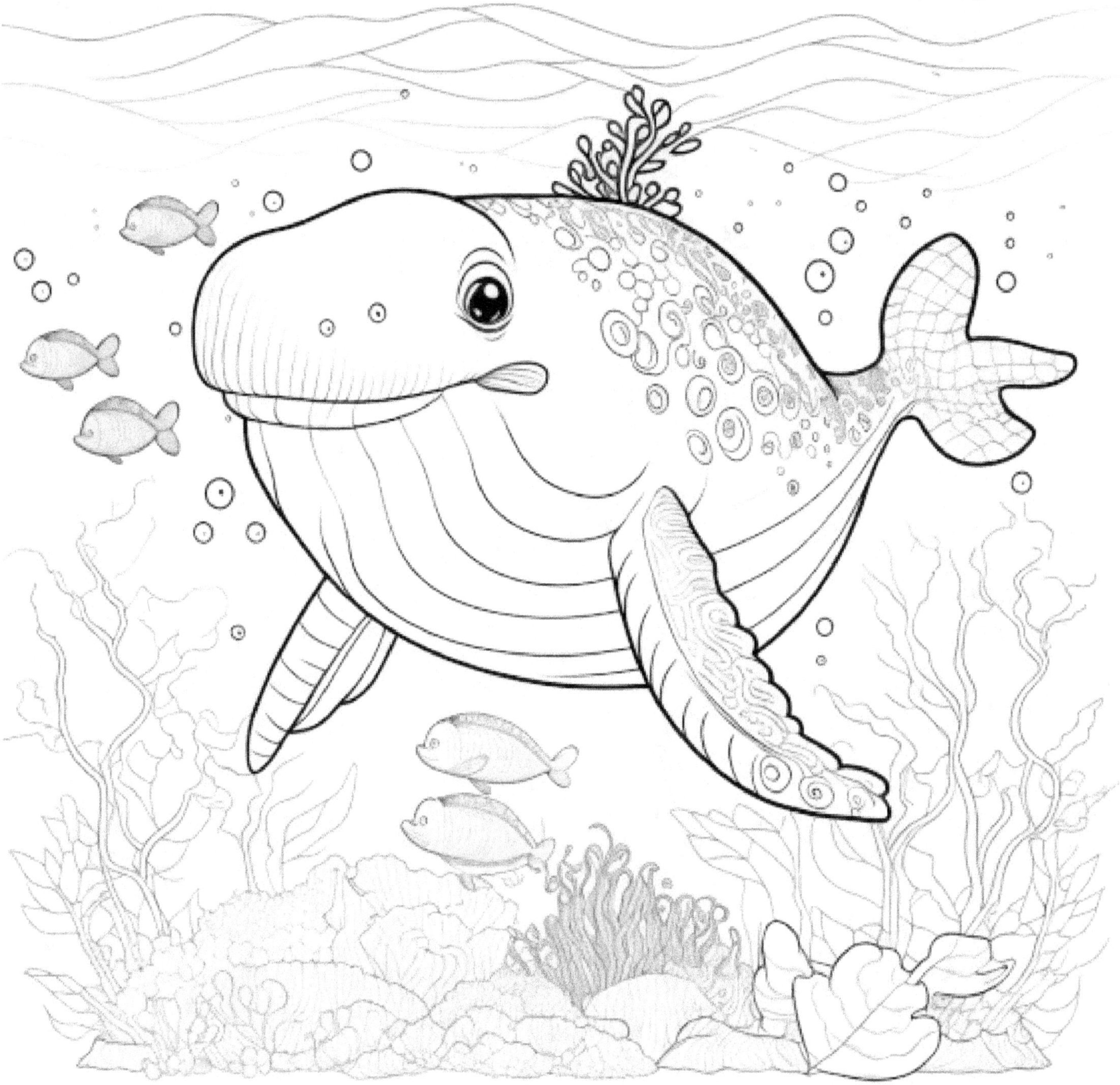

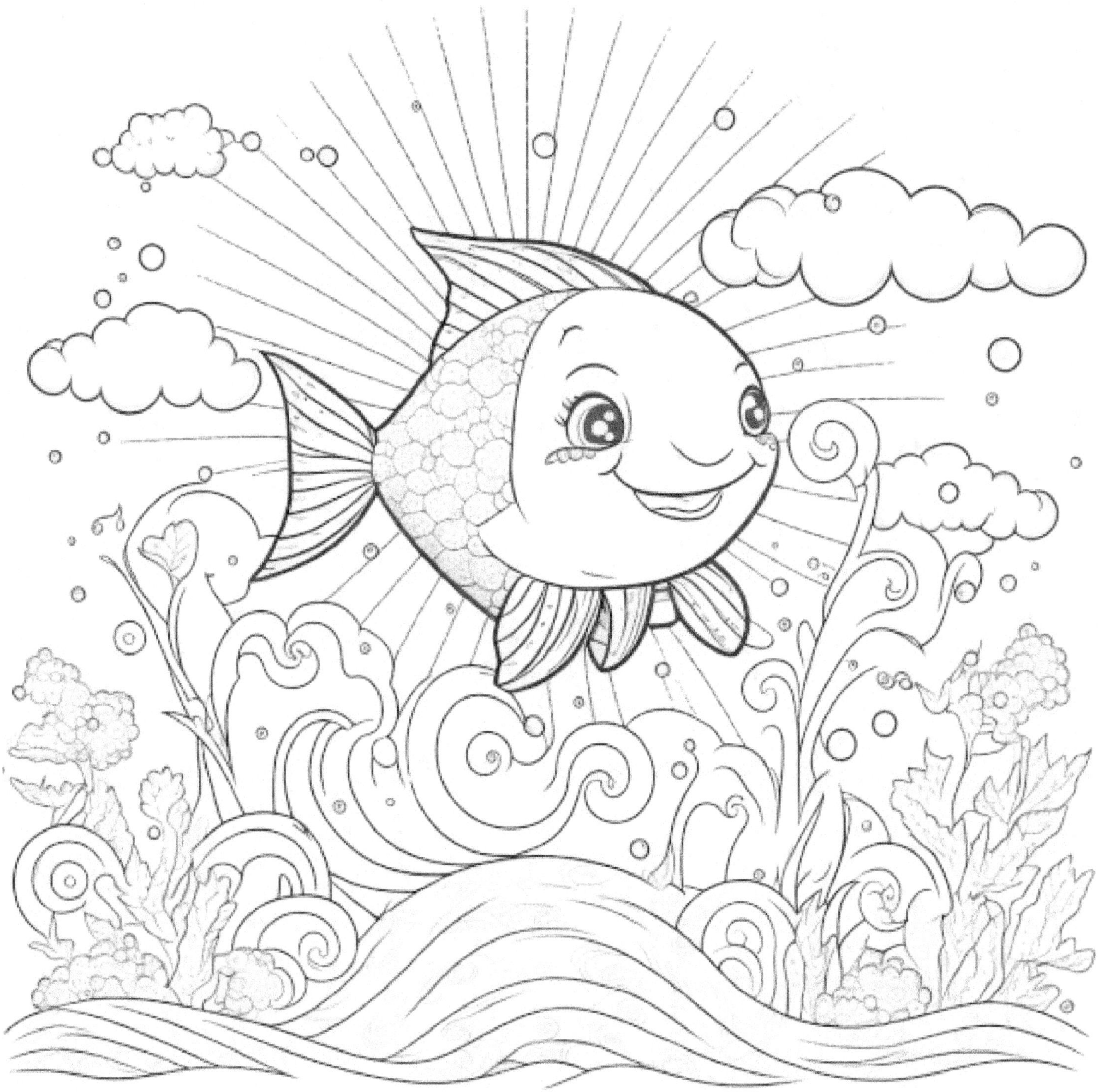

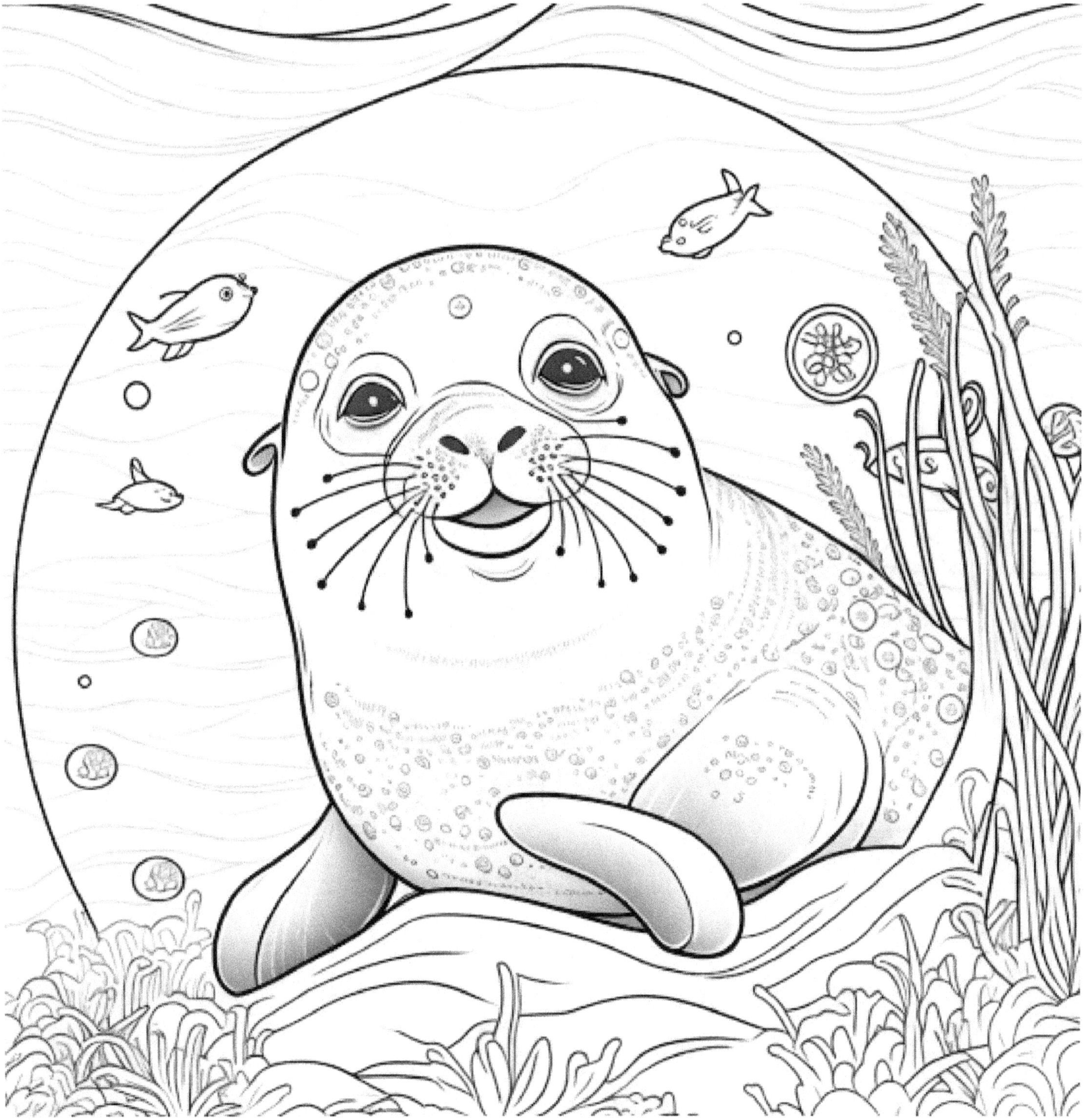

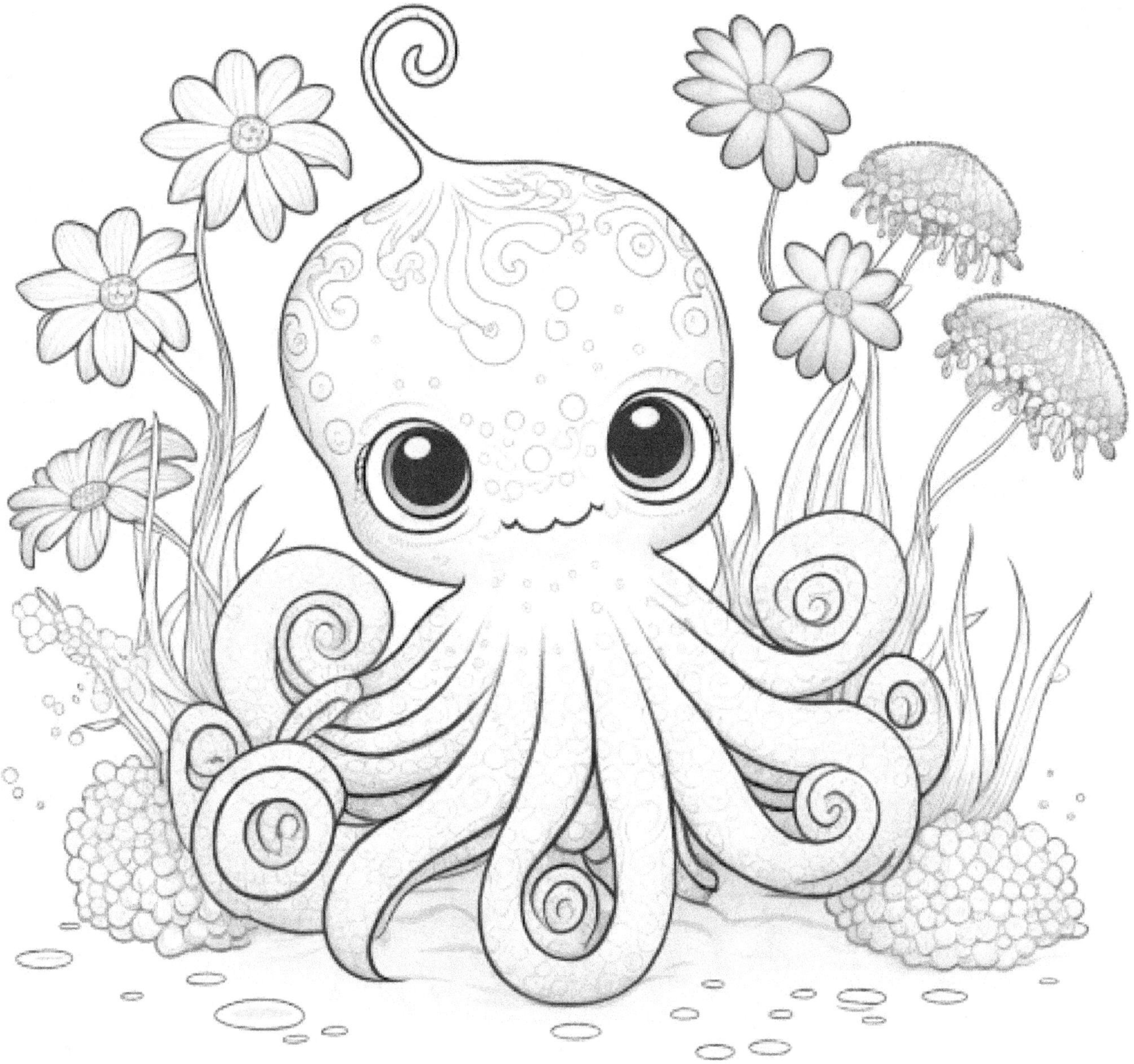

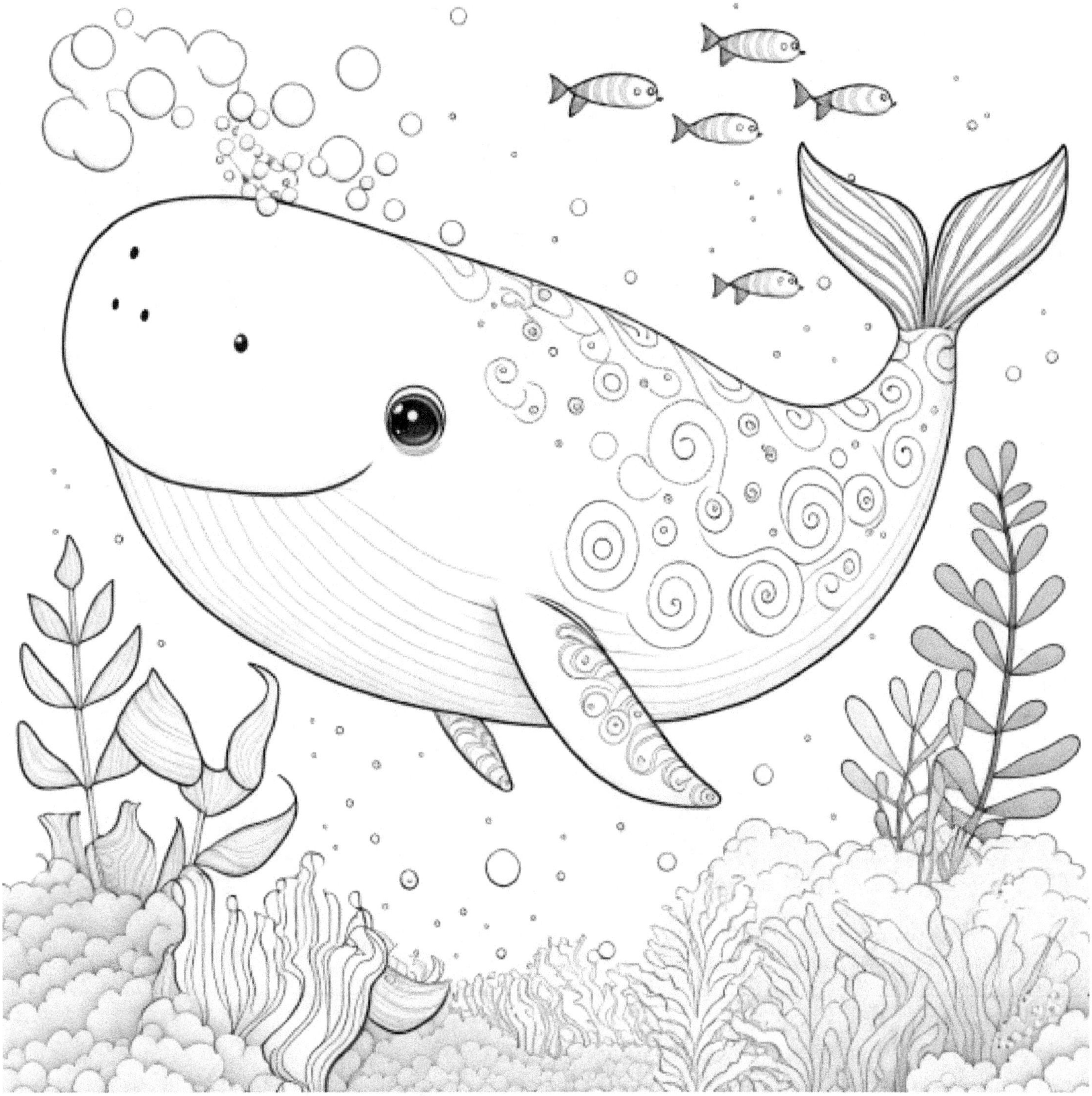

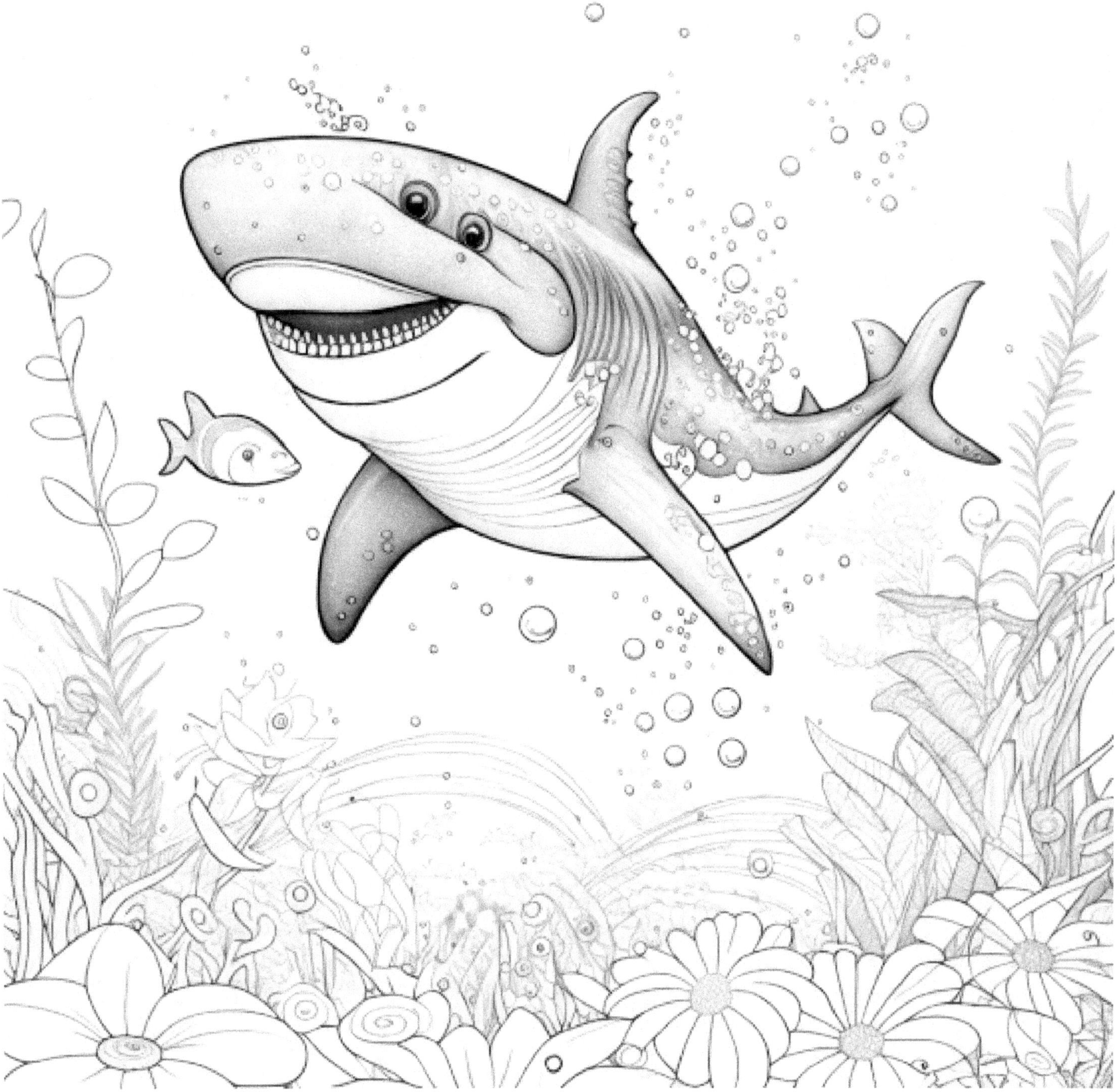

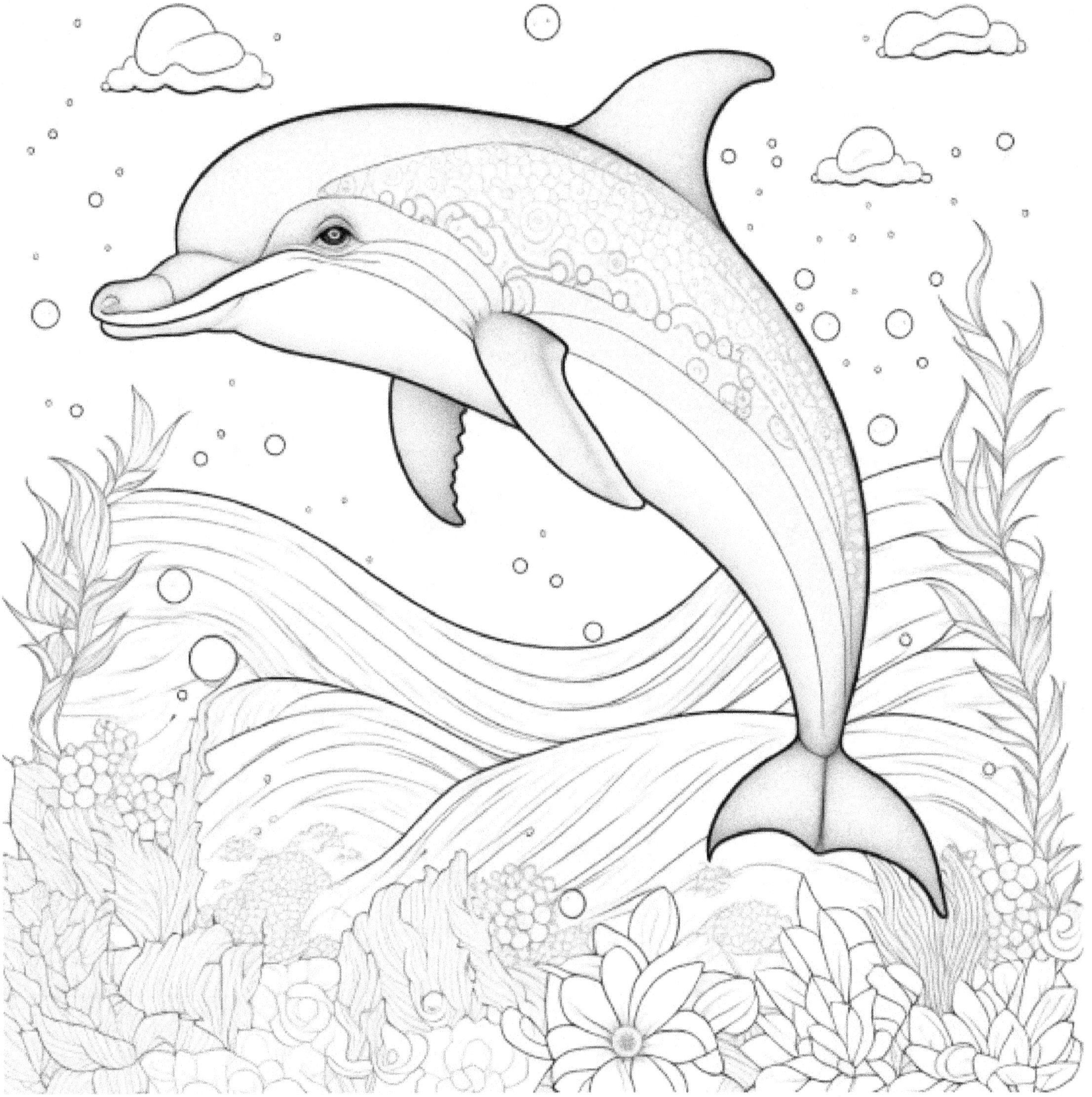

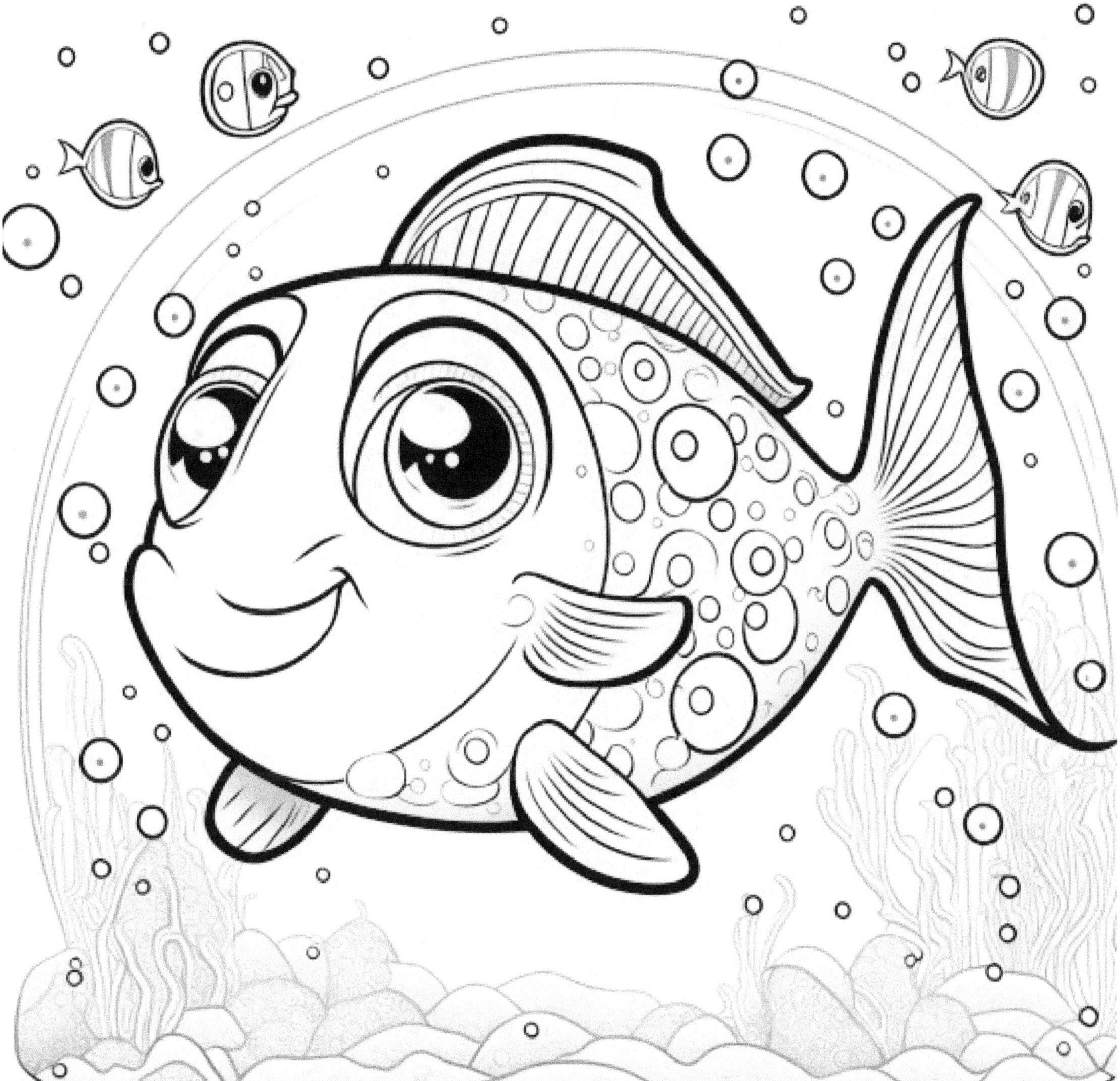

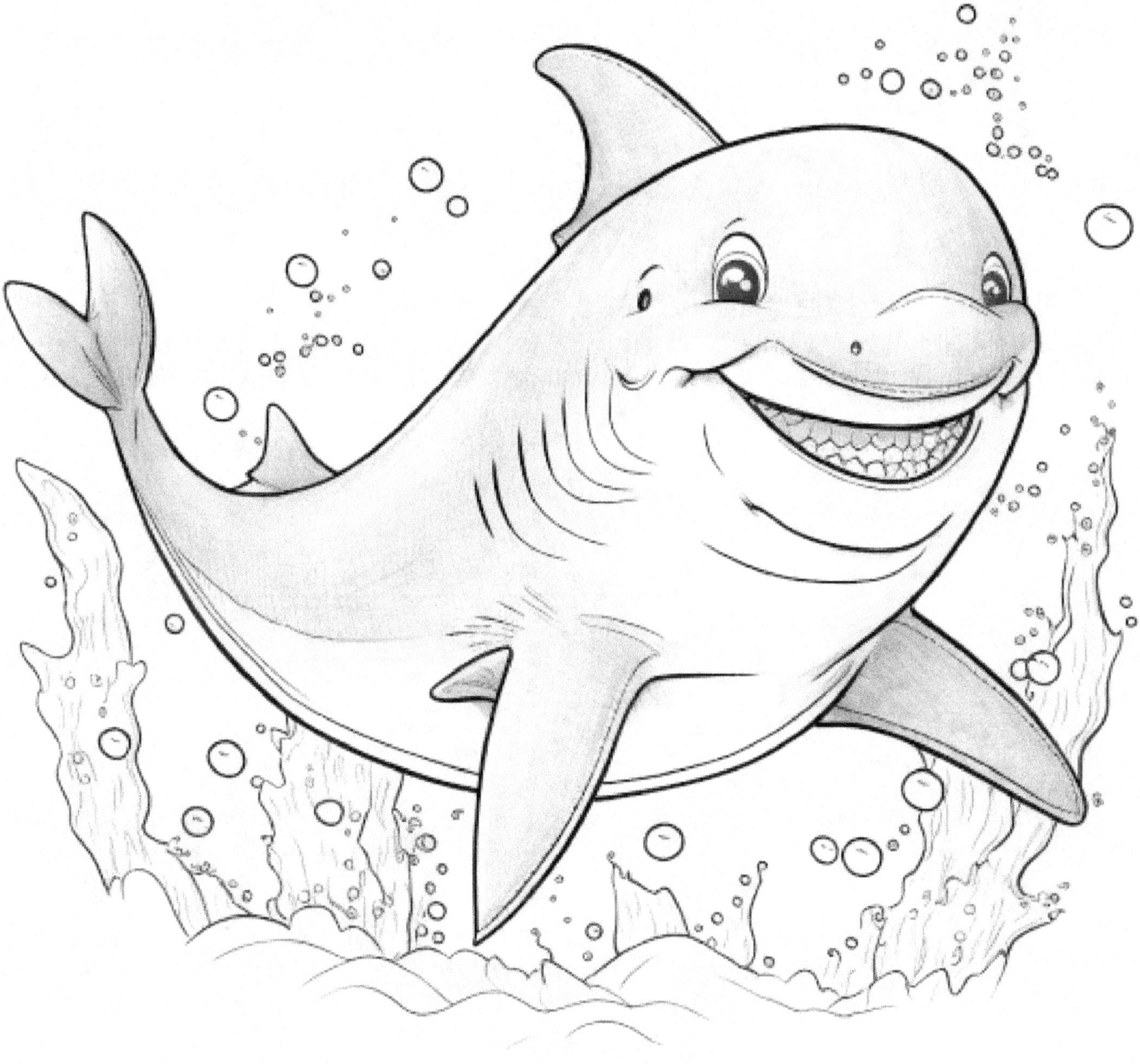

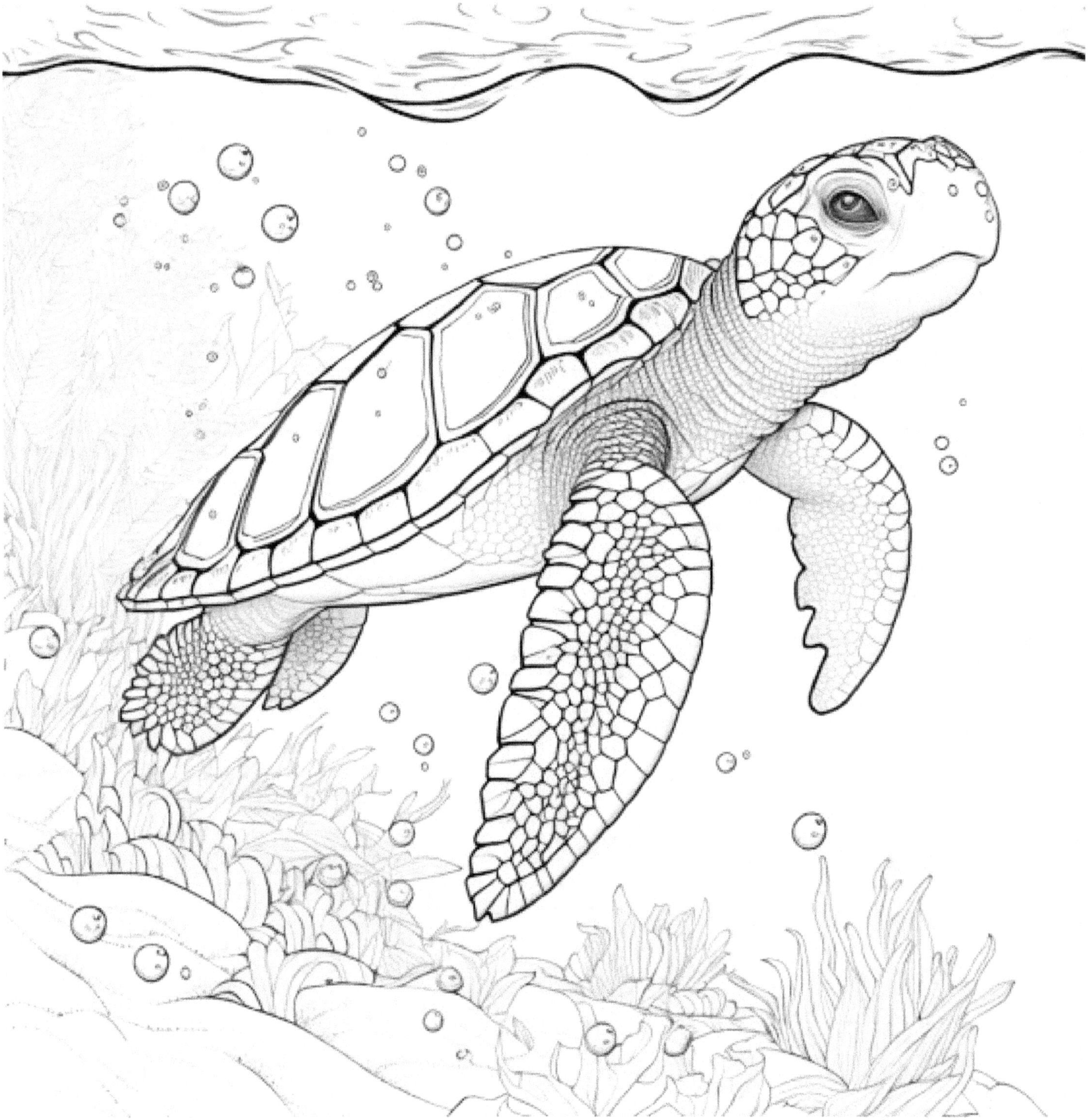

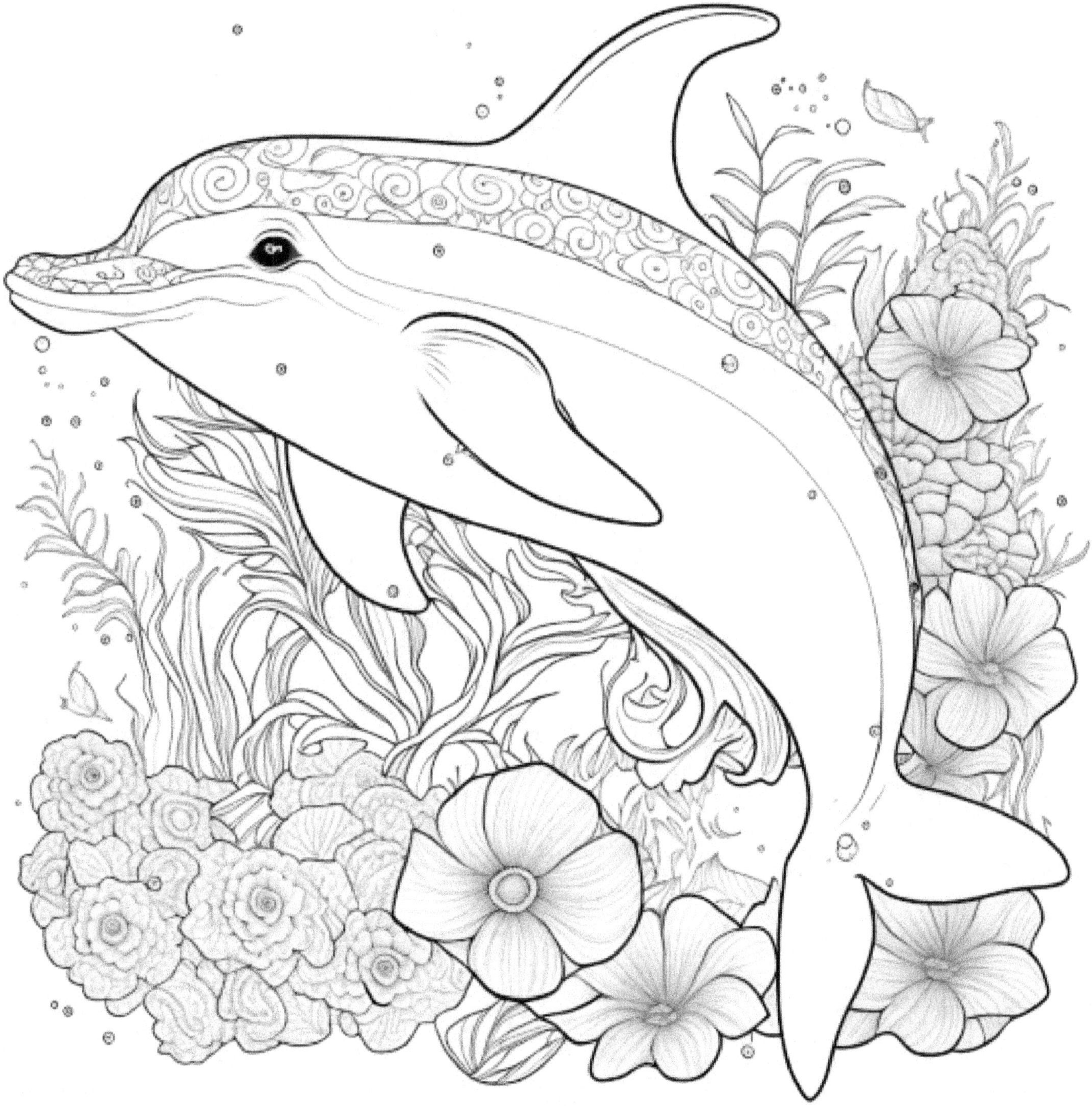

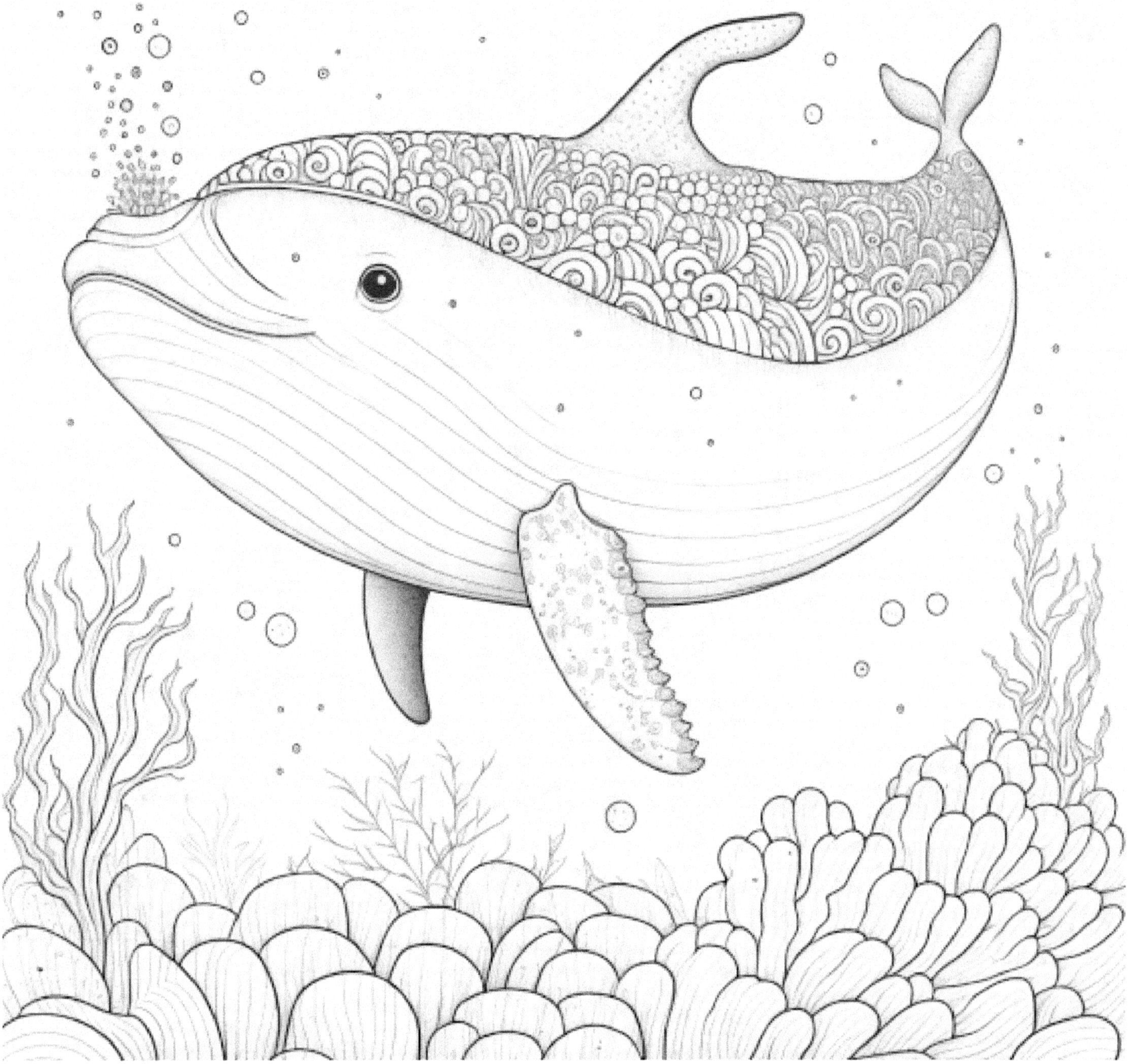

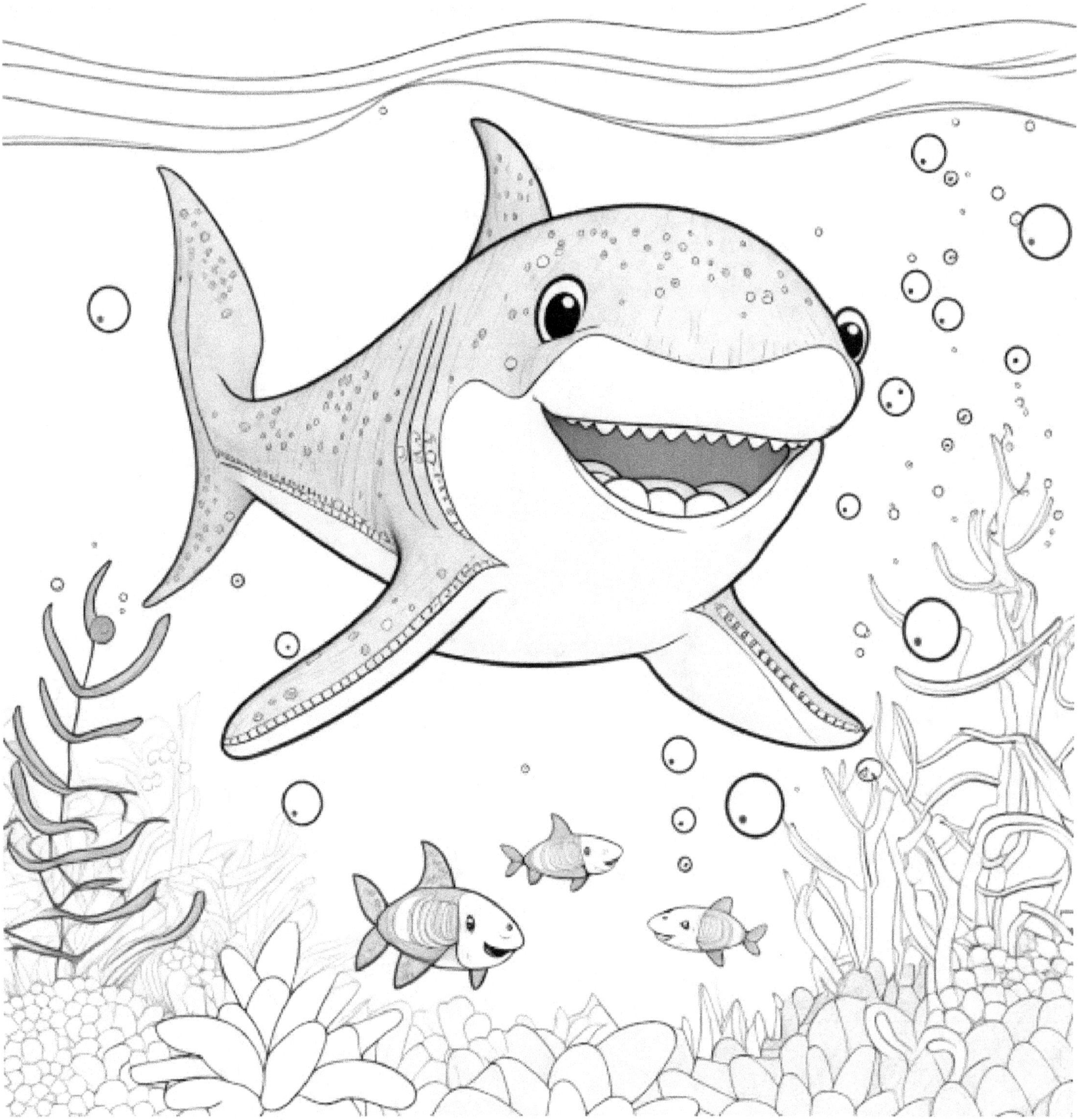

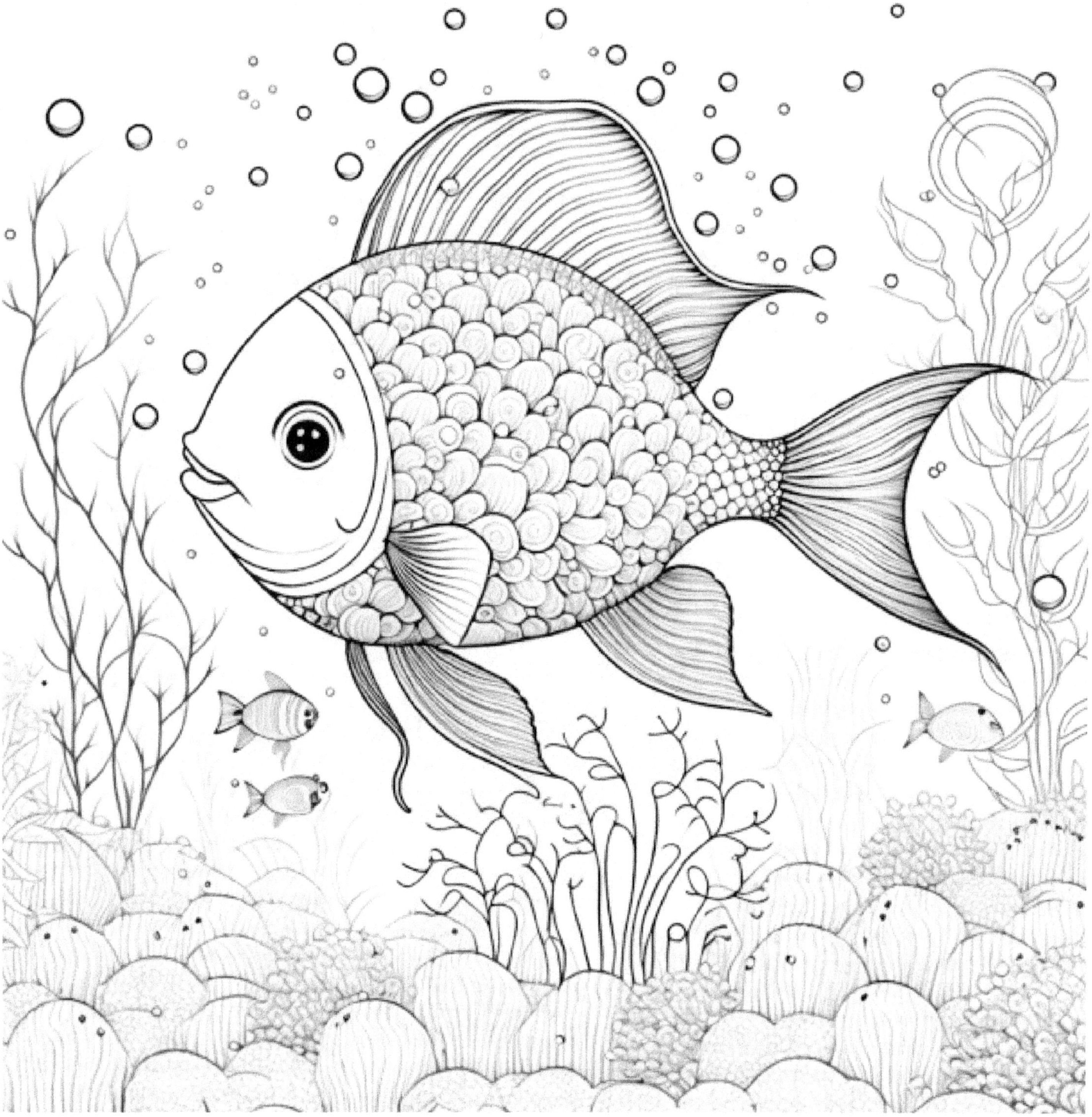

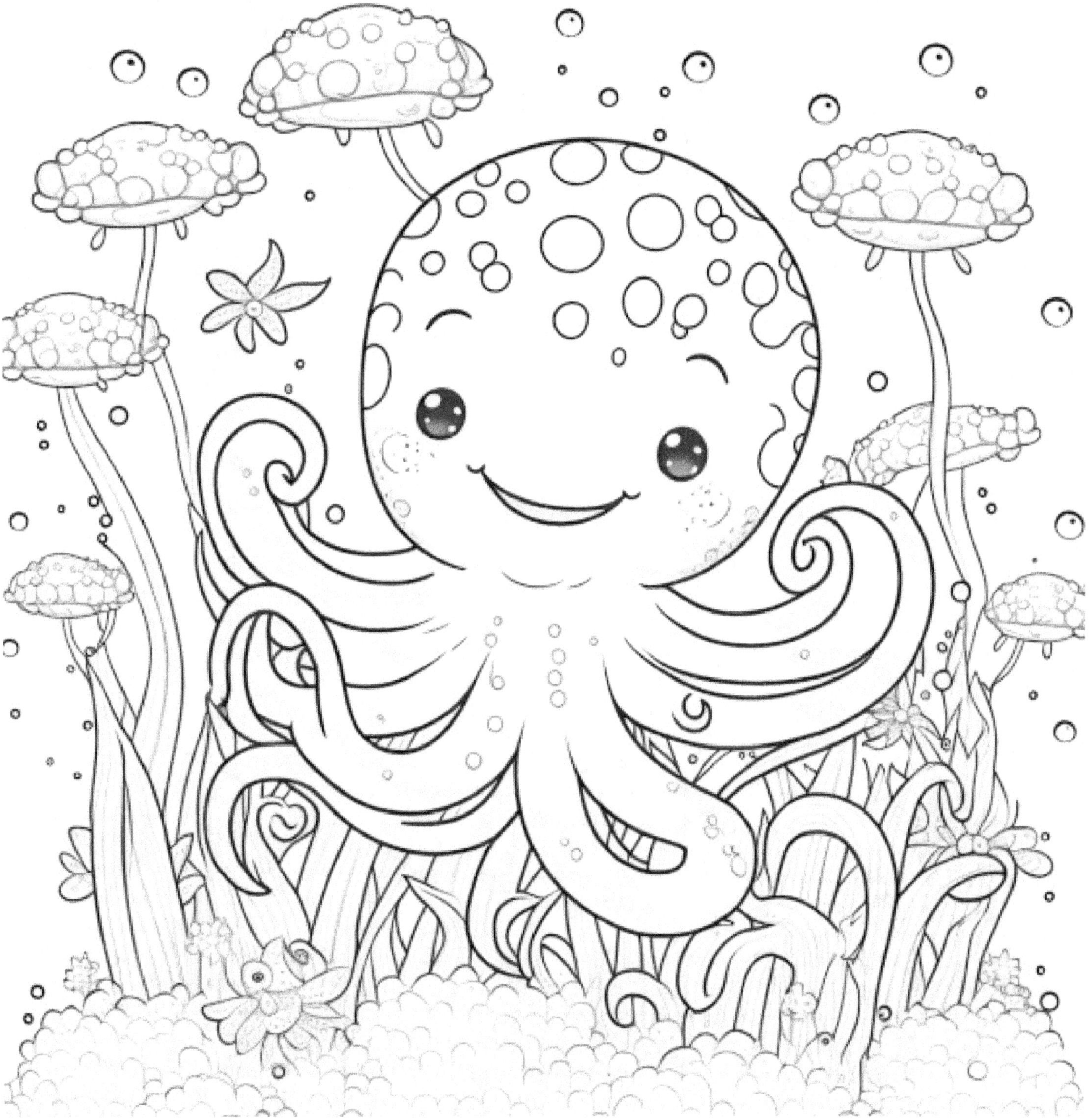

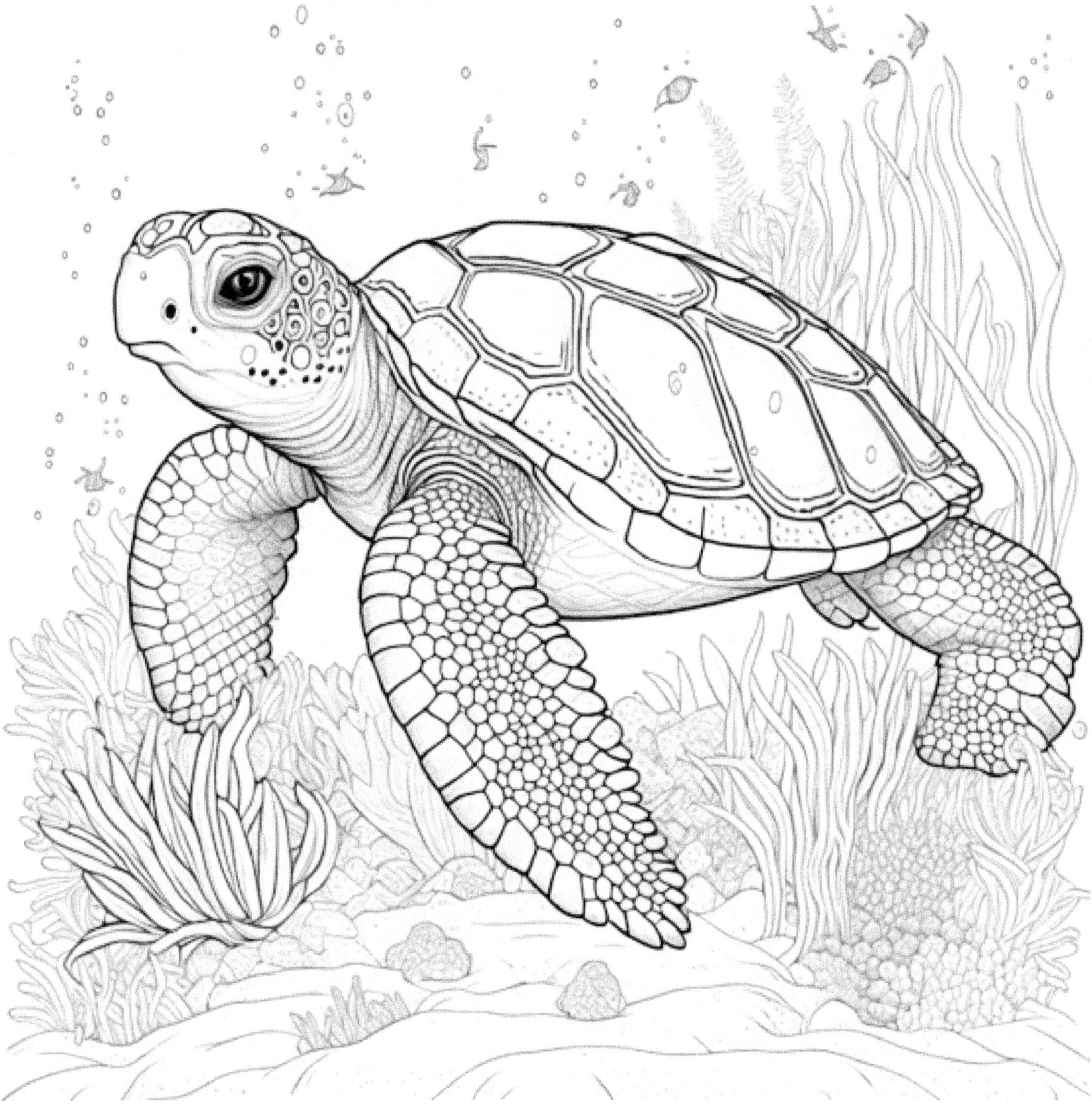

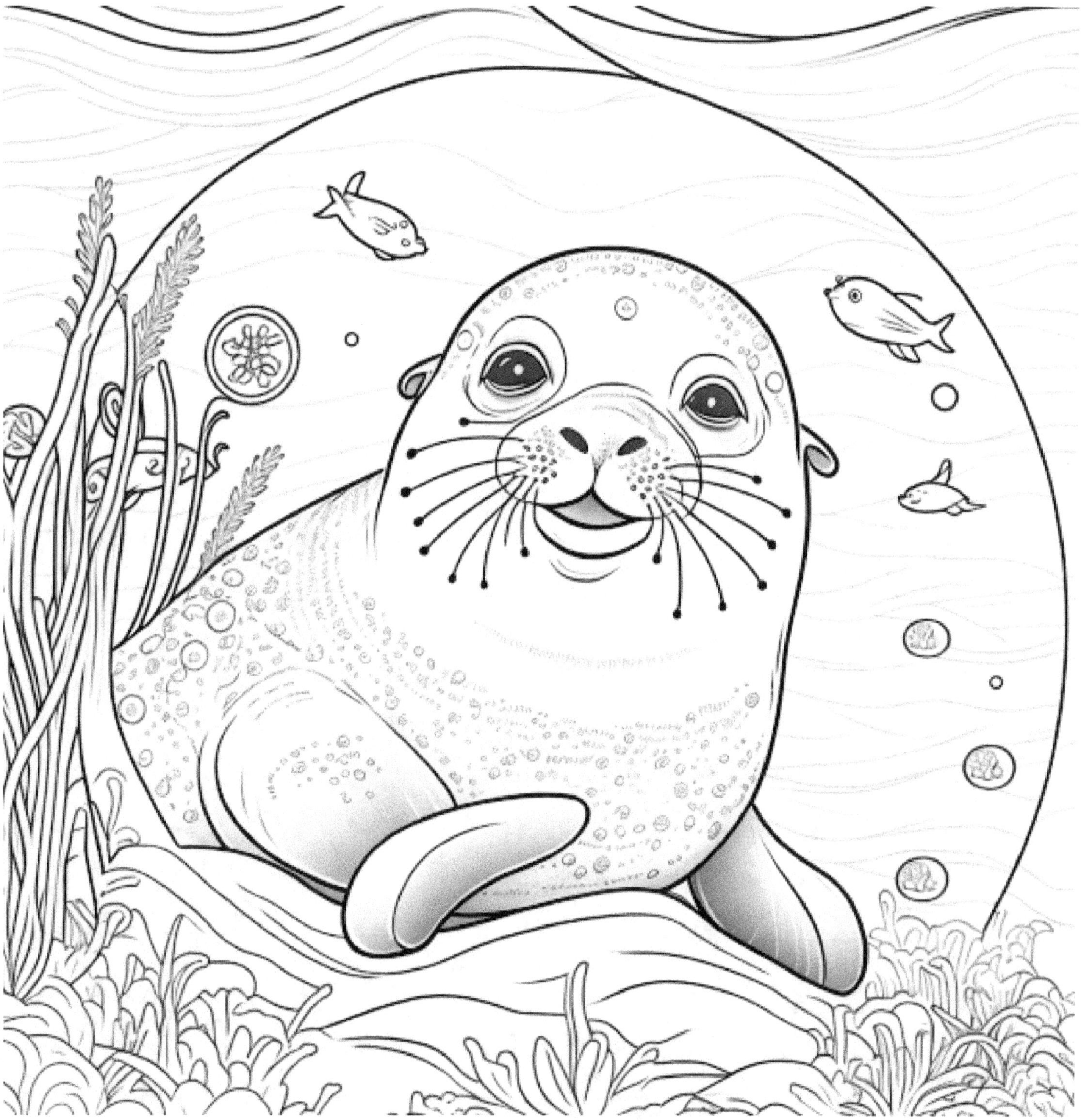

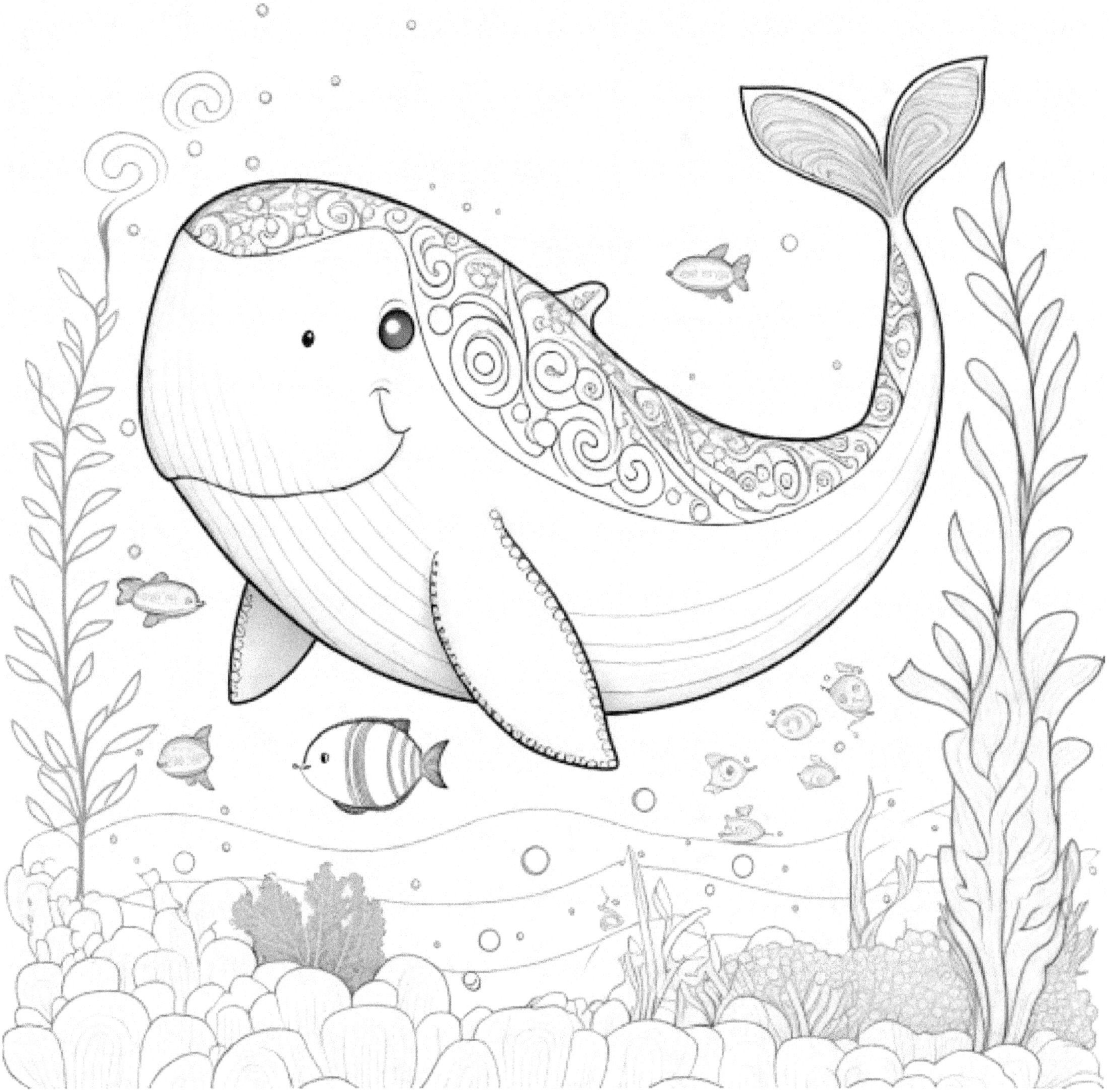

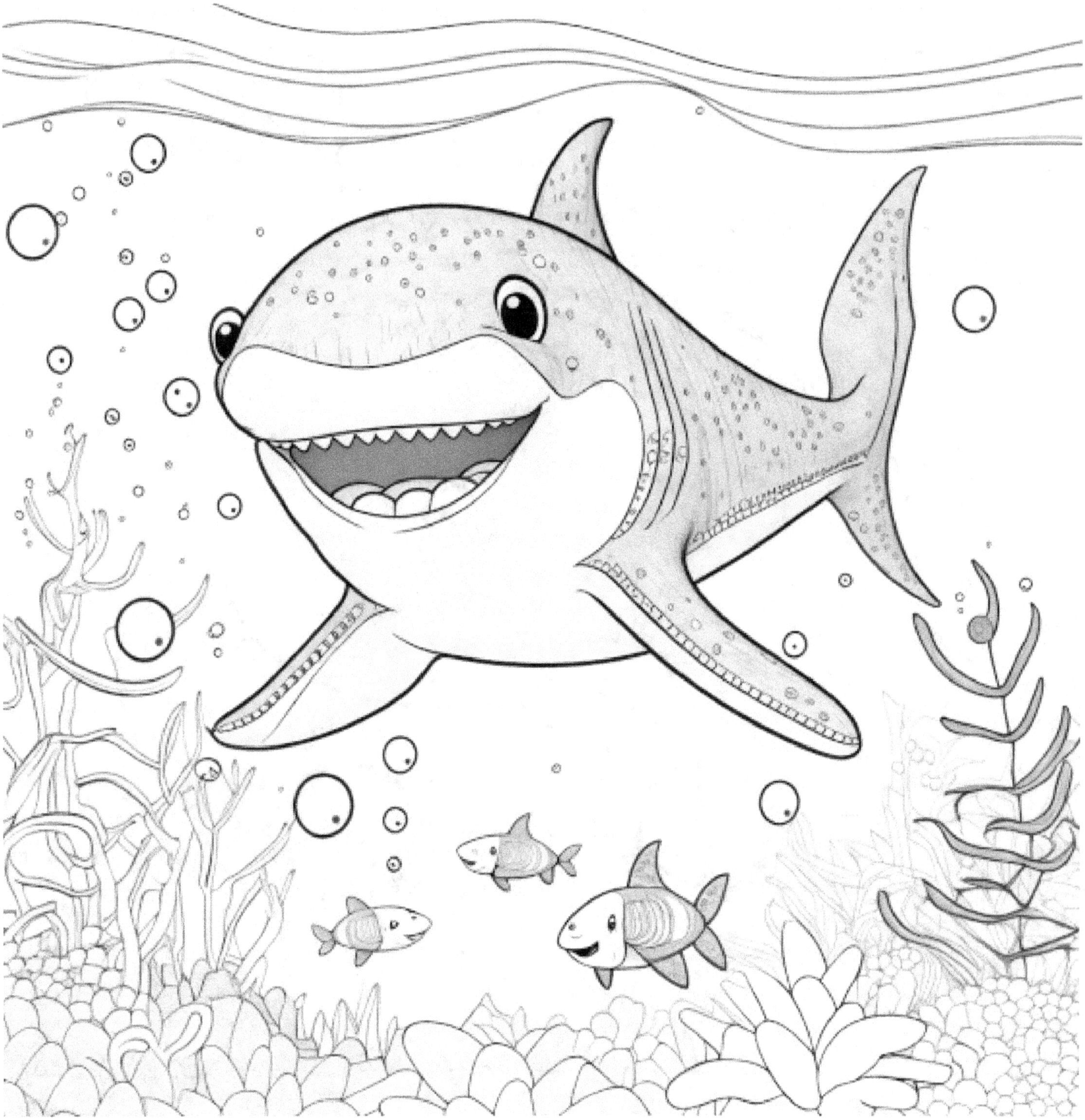

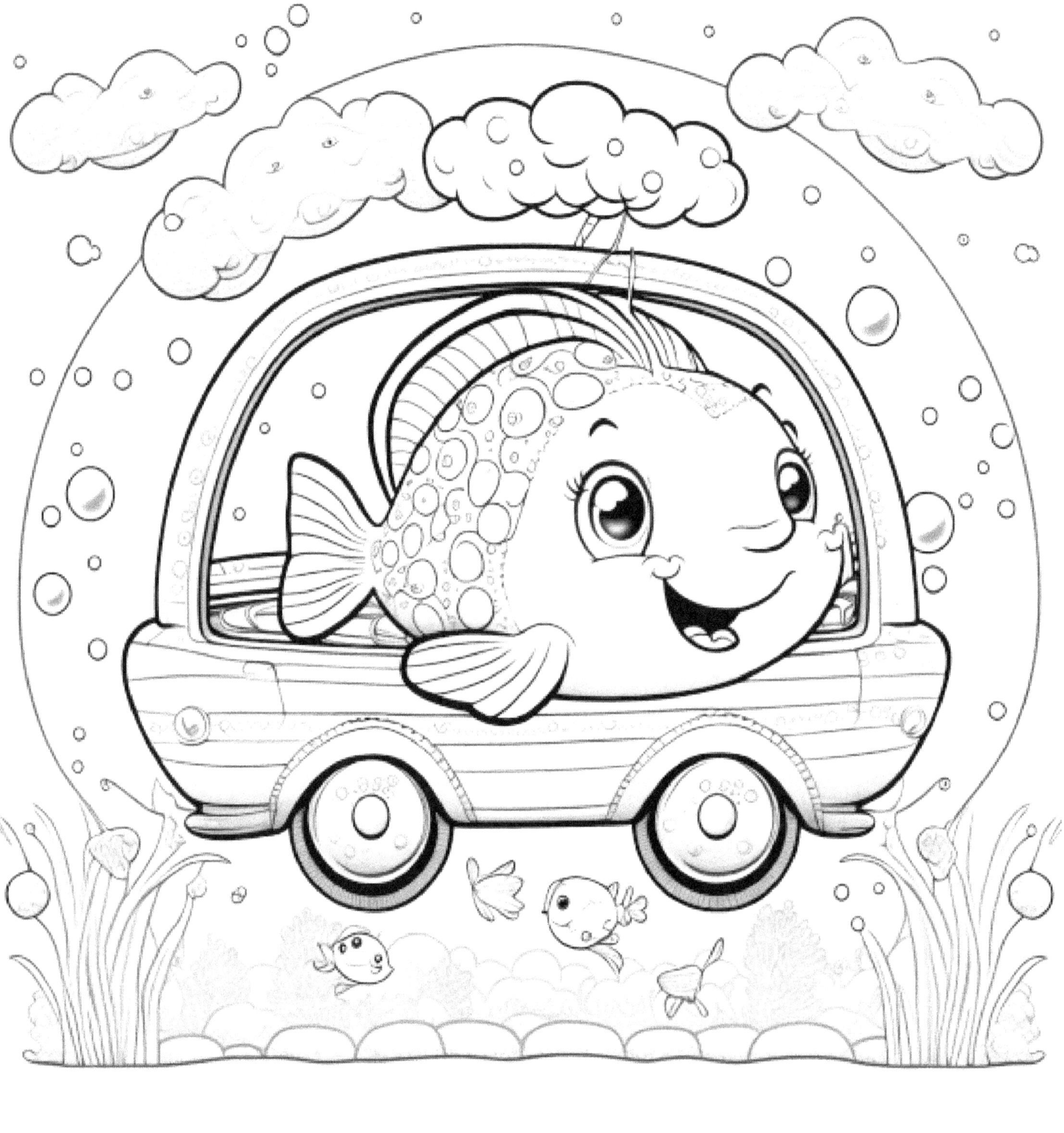

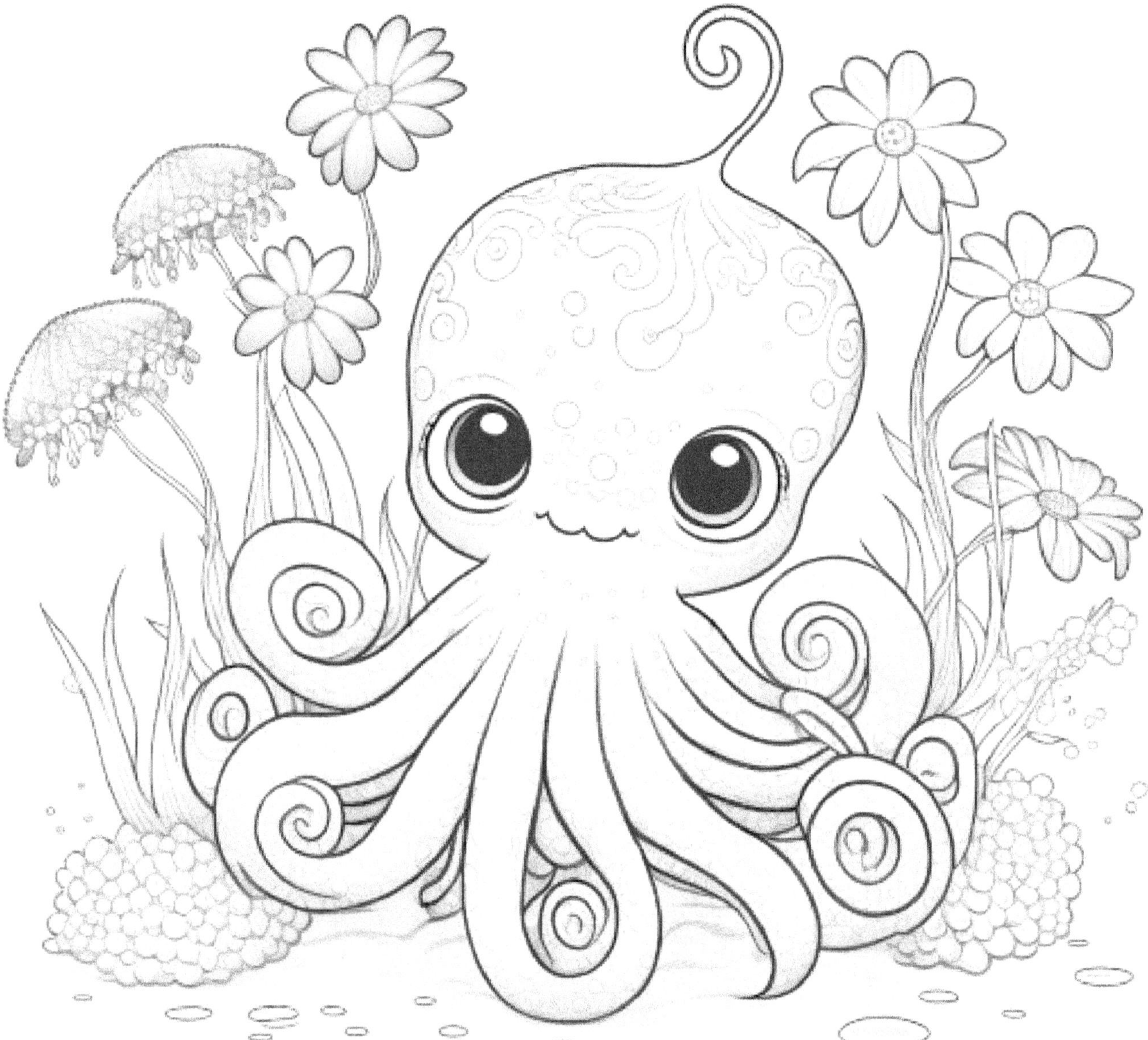

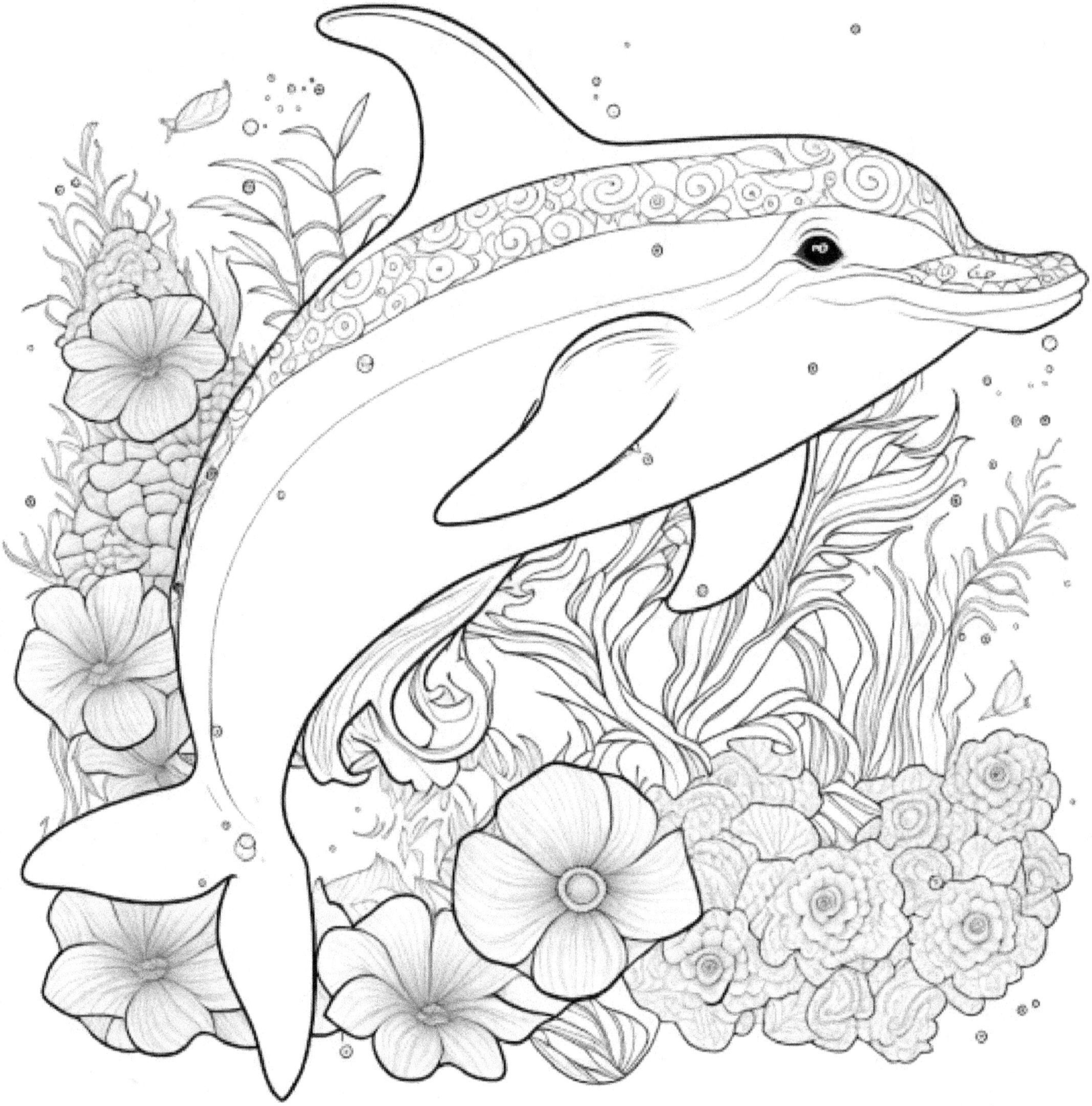

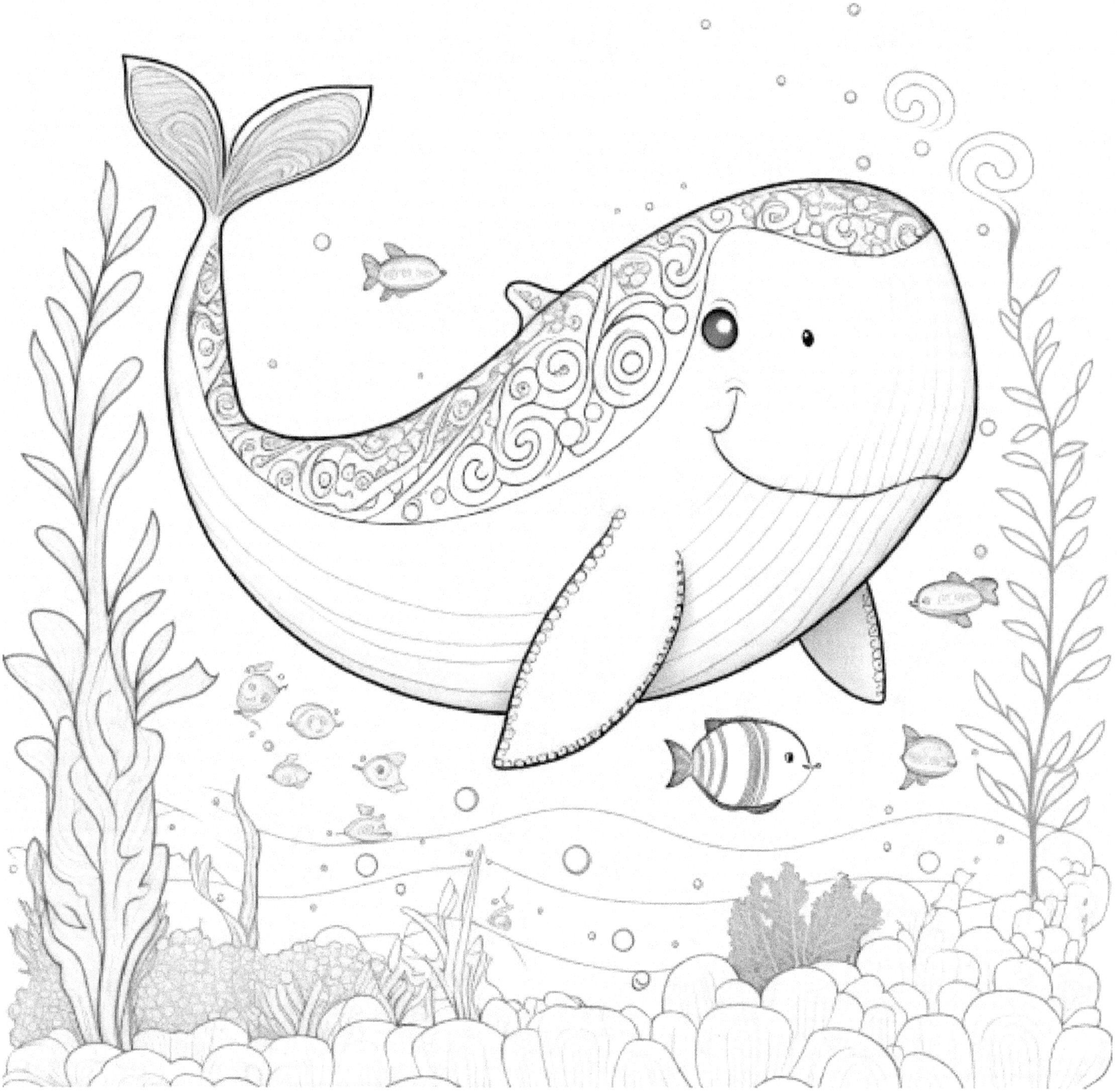

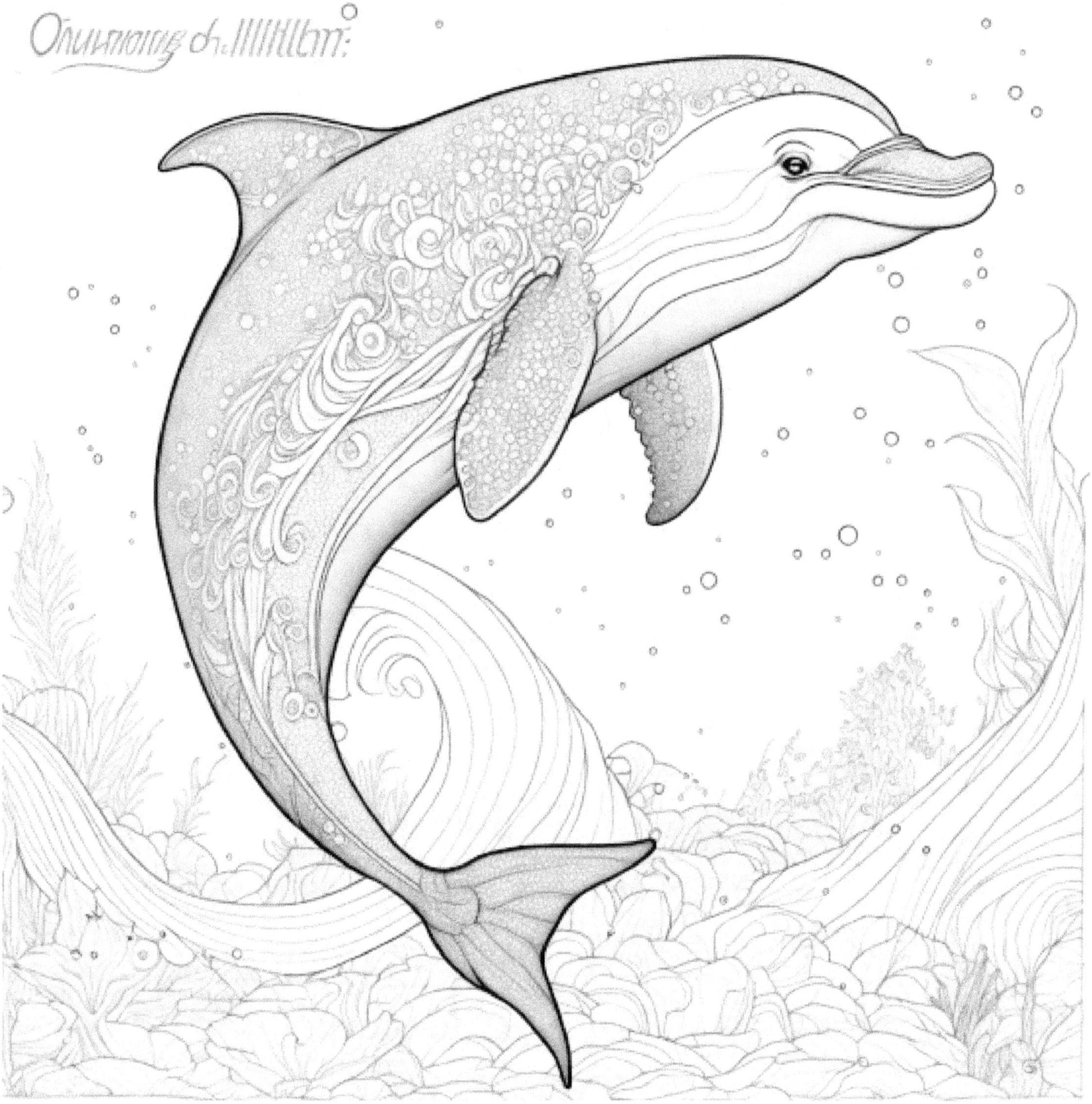

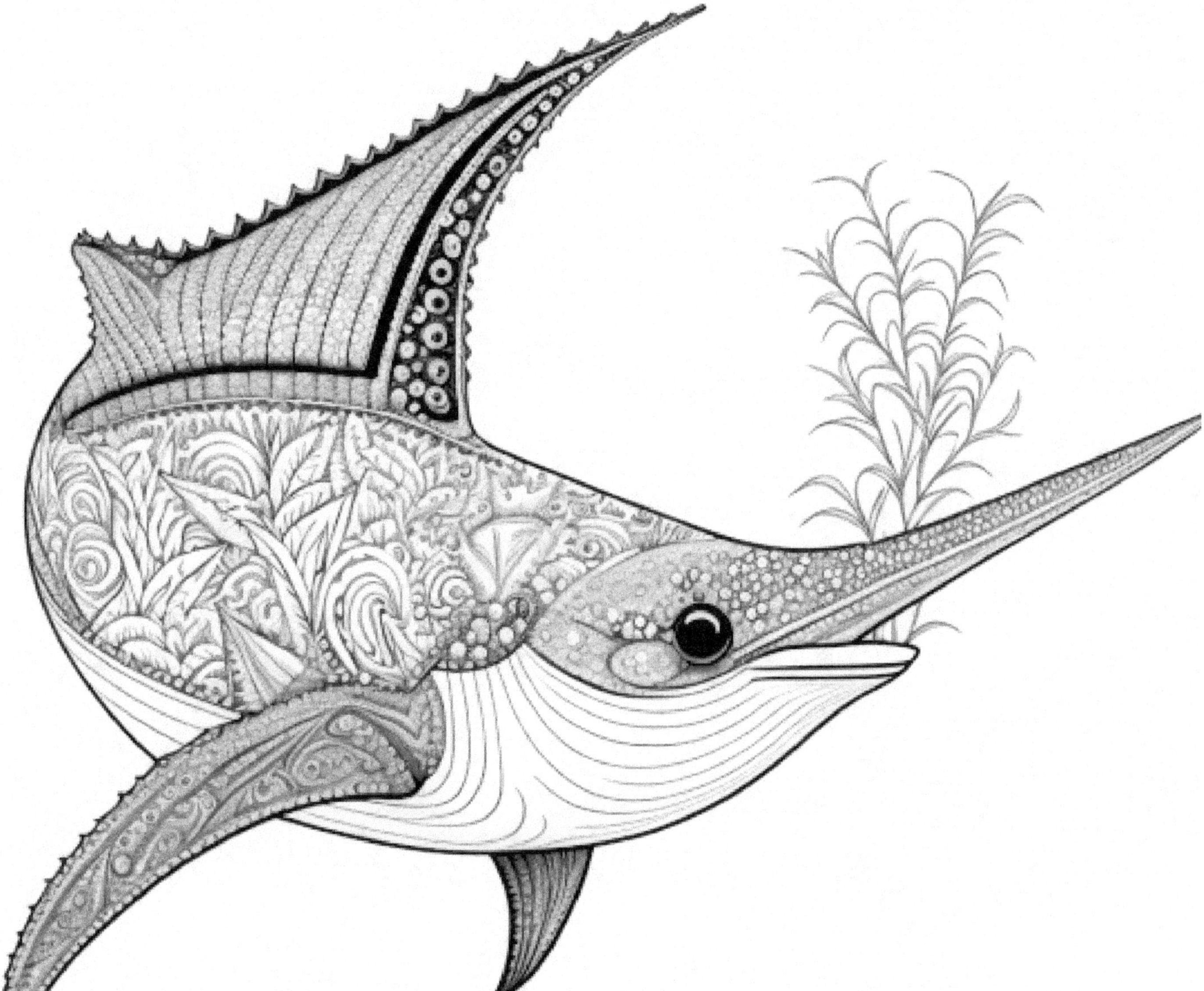

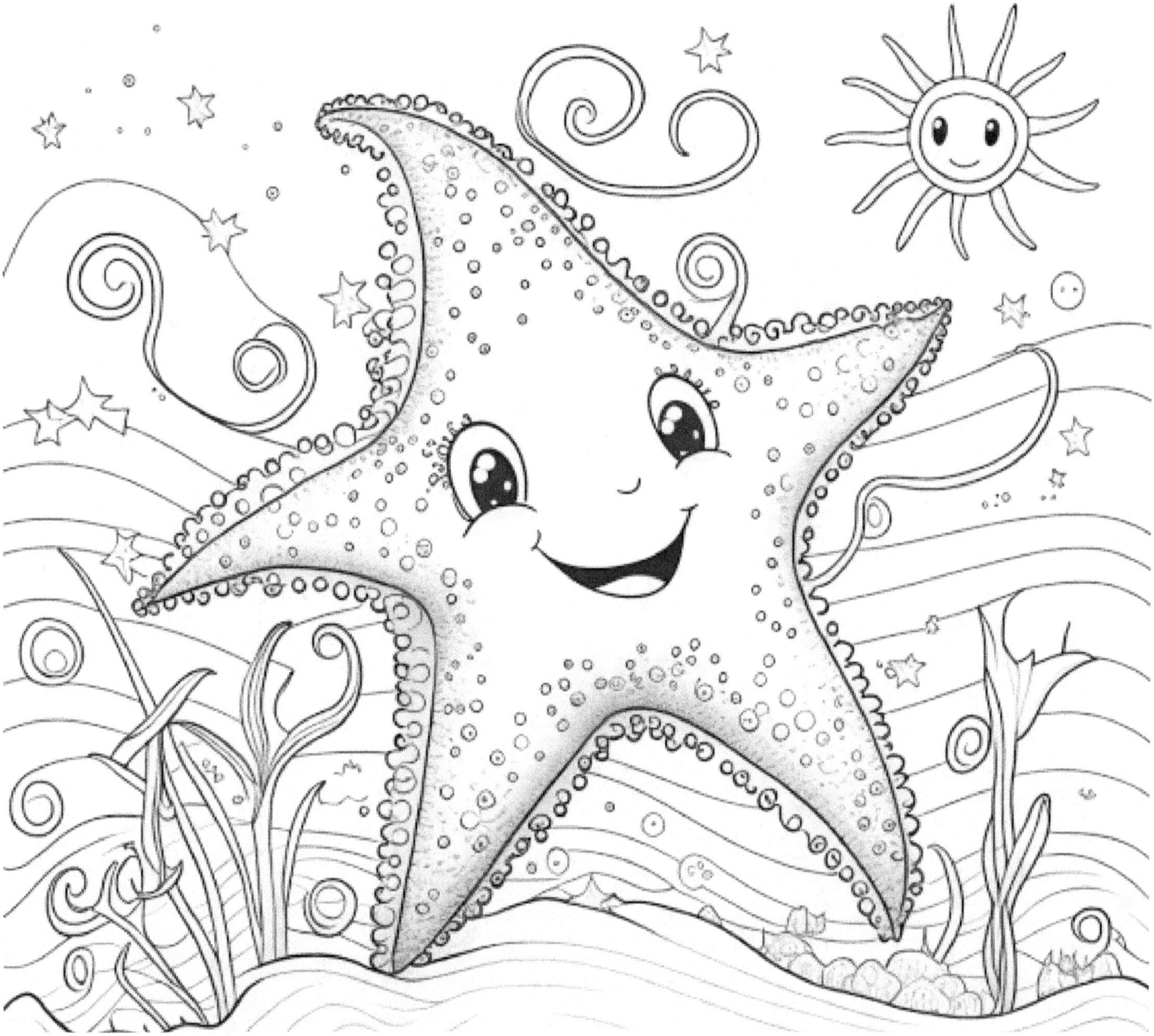

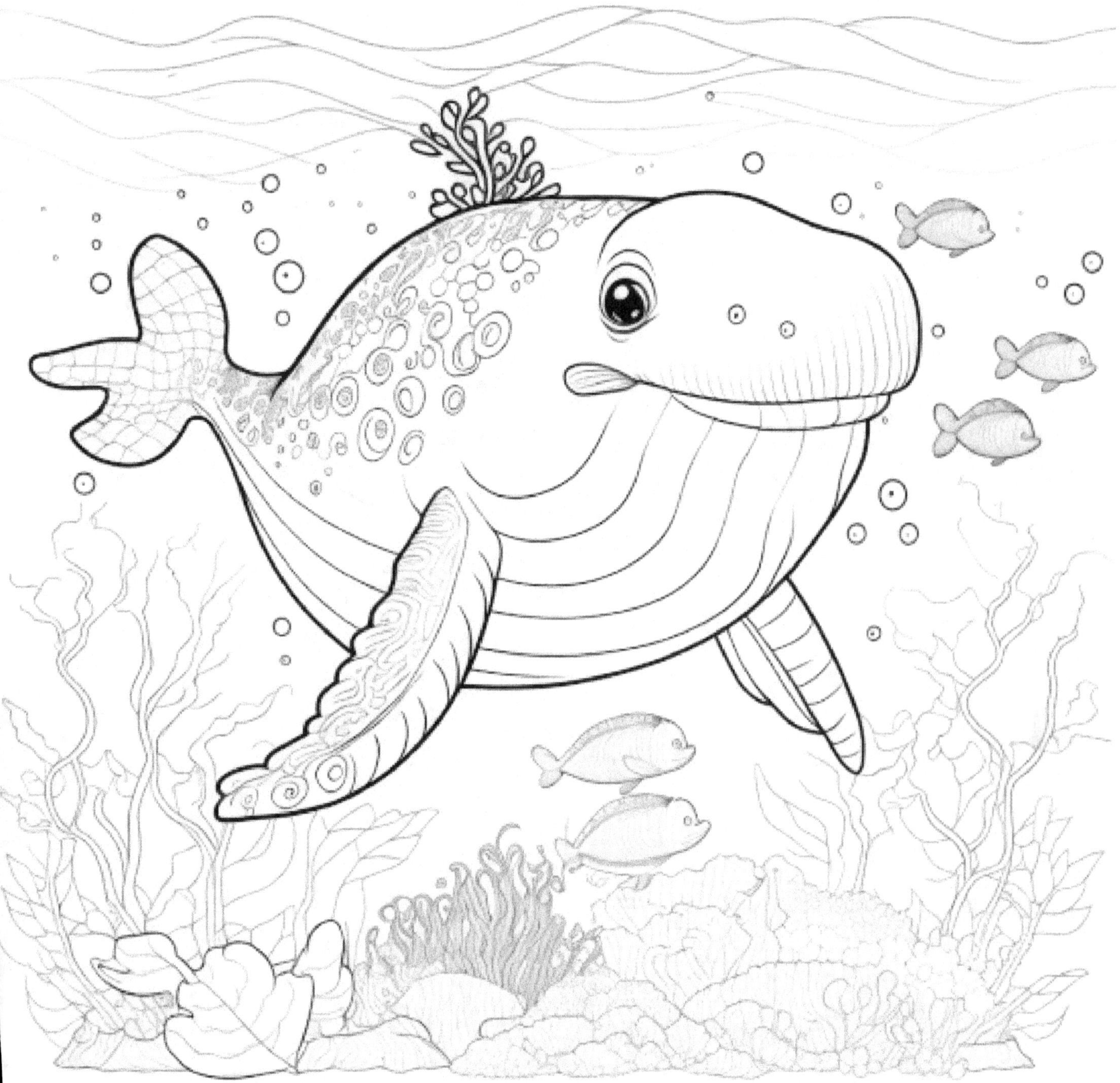

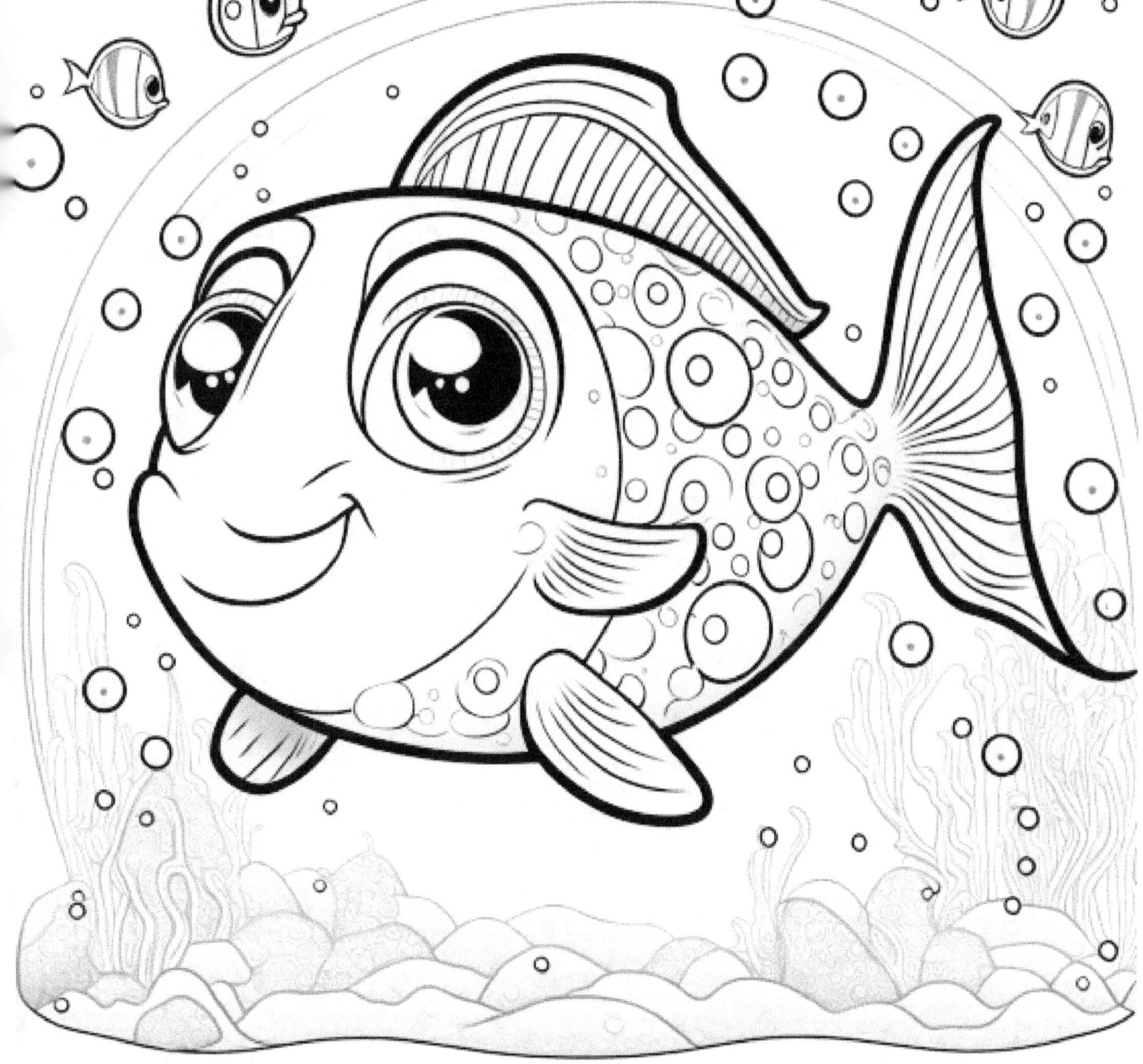

www.ingramcontent.com/pod-product-compliance
Lightning Source LLC
Chambersburg PA
CBHW081512220526
45467CB00010B/2889
* 9 7 9 8 3 8 9 5 8 3 0 3 0 *